D0291813

**Outtatown
Resource Book**

AHER AROP BOL

The Lost Boy

Aher Arop Bol

Kwela Books

Kwela Books,
an imprint of NB Publishers,
40 Heerengracht, Cape Town, South Africa
PO Box 6525, Roggebaai, 8012, South Africa
http://www.kwela.com

Copyright © 2009 Aher Arop Bol

All rights reserved
No part of this book may be reproduced or
transmitted in any form or by any electronic
or mechanical means, including photocopying
and recording, or by any other information
storage or retrieval system, without written
permission from the publisher

Cover design by Michiel Botha
Cover photograph by Tolga Kostak
Maps by Bennie Krüger
Typography by Nielfa Cassiem-Carelse
Set in Zapf
Printed and bound by Paarl Print,
Oosterland Street, Paarl, South Africa

First edition, first impression 2009

ISBN: 978-0-7957-0278-5

I dedicate this book to
Dut Mayout, my cousin,
and to the other boys who, like him,
did not survive

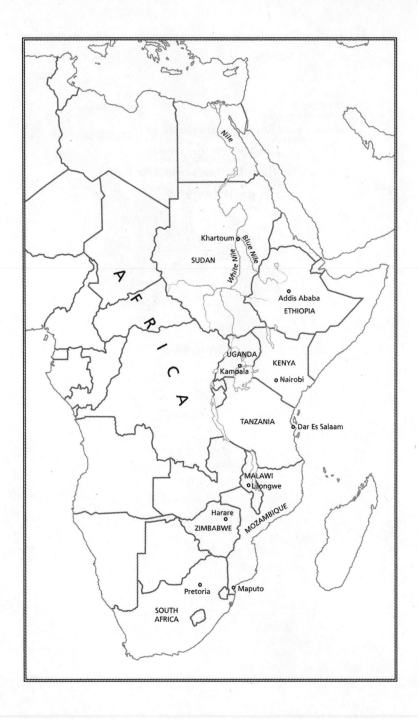

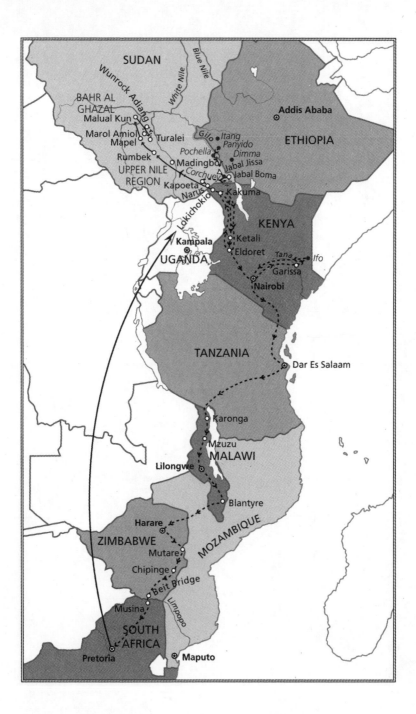

Prologue

What is the price of freedom? How many lives does it take to buy liberty in Sudan, where religion and politics breed war and poverty, where Muslim Arabs from the north are fighting a war against the people of the south – the animists and the Christians?

It was on 16 May 1983, in the town of Madingbor, that a hundred and five men, the founders of the Sudanese People's Liberation Army (SPLA), took up arms against the Islamic government in the north. This was the beginning of a war in which two-and-a-half million lives have been lost, thousands of orphans abandoned and prosperity and dignity ravaged.

This is where my unfortunate peers and I were born – in the rift caused by war – and where we grew up – in the crossfire. We were victims and targets. There were eighteen thousand of us, but each suffered in isolation, without parents to help us deal with the corpses we were too weak to bury.

Watched by a world that no longer recognised the value of human life and dignity, the government forces treated the southerners inhumanly, robbing them not only of their possessions, but also of their children and their lives.

It is suffering and frustration that have compelled me to write this book – the story of my youth – and the need to plead with the mediators to not only *end* the war in Sudan, but to *solve* the issues behind it. I pray that God will make this possible, so that the people may return and live in peace once again.

This book is about my experiences and those of other minors in Panyido and other refugee camps. It tells of the agony, the hunger, disease and thirst we survived, of the relief and camaraderie we found during periods of rest, of our search for meaning and for ways in which to make this world a better place to live in.

War has scattered us to all corners of Sudan and across the world. We have learned to put our trust in God. And we honour the memory of our elders who took responsibility for us in the camps and warzones, even though they themselves were suffering.

In Sudan, land of corruption,
the voices that once spoke for us have now fallen silent

From a song sung in Dinka by Deng Kout
(also known as Deng Pannon)

PART 1

1

I arrived at a refugee camp in Ethiopia on the shoulders of my uncle Atem, who had cleared a way for us through the bush as we fled. I soon learned that the camp was called Panyido. It was 1987 and I was three or four years old.

Later, when I returned to Sudan, I discovered that Panyido was a two-day journey (if you walked day and night) from the Sudanese border, and many, many days' walk from my village.

It was night when my uncle and I, and my two older cousins, Dut and Yaac, reached the banks of the Tana River, where the camp was situated. There were throngs of people who, like us, had been told by the villagers we had met along the way that food and shelter might be found there.

New arrivals, who had suffered hunger, thirst, disease and injuries on their travels, rushed expectantly to the centre of the camp, but there was nothing for them. As they had forced their weak bodies to march along the river towards the camp, rumours of food and medical attention had given them hope. They had imagined being welcomed in true Sudanese style by missing family members who would offer them something to eat, or by strangers who might be persuaded to share the food they had, but in Panyido there was nothing but more hungry faces and people crying for help. There were no food supplies and no relief workers. Some, covered in white dust, sank helplessly to the ground and remained there; others, who still had the strength, turned towards the seemingly endless stream of people who kept coming from the bush and helped them across the river.

The days went by and hundreds of new refugees arrived, but no assistance came from the Ethiopian government or the United Nations High Commisioner for Refugees (UNHCR) – despite the rumours that relief workers would come with food and medicine as soon as they were able to. As their hunger increased some, who hadn't eaten for many days, gathered the strength to go hunting. A few others, those who had the energy to walk to the nearest villages, returned with the meagre supplies they had exchanged items of clothing for.

In Panyido there was only one red-dust road, which linked it to Itang, another camp, where the first refugees had settled. All eyes remained on this road, but the hoped-for roar of truck engines did not come. So every man had to deal with the suffering and disease of his own family by himself.

Panyido was hot. I remember the shadows under the trees. They were thick with bodies. Living bodies. And dead bodies.

My uncle Atem and I found a spot under a marula tree, where we took shelter from the fierce sun. At night we followed the others to the open ground to bed down. Some people, however, were too frail to move away from the trees. In the morning the dead were carried away to be buried.

I missed my mother and my father and didn't understand why they weren't with me in the camp. I saw the eyes of a dead man looking straight at me. They were large and bright, but could not see.

Months passed, but no food arrived. There were no longer enough people left with the strength to go hunting to save the lives of the starving. Then one morning, a little help came from some Ethiopian soldiers. Thousands heard the roar of a tractor approaching. It was a green-and-black striped tractor, pulling a red trailer with bags of maize on it.

Food! There were cries of agony and cries of joy!

When the tractor stopped, hundreds of hands grasped. Maize from shattered bags spilled onto the road. Strong men grabbed hold of the bags. Let the weak pick up from the ground – even if it meant that they were trampled to death in the rush to reach the food. Crawling men and women ate the maize raw. The sick were begging to be fed. One man was given some kernels but was unable to chew them. He gave up and died, his family wailing at his agony.

That day three loads were delivered, and this continued for a week – a blessing that turned into a curse. Eating so recklessly after months of starvation caused severe thirst and people rushed to the river. Some were so weak that as they knelt down to drink they toppled over and drowned. Cholera killed many more as by then the water had been polluted by the sick and the dead.

2

God alone knows how I escaped death in that camp.

My uncle Atem survived too – the uncle who had carried me all the way to the camp. He took responsibility for me and made rules I was not allowed to break. "When you are very thirsty," he cautioned, "don't drink more than a small mouthful when we get to water."

He told me to drink water only when he would provide it – usually three times a day: in the morning, the afternoon and the evening. I was not allowed to drink the water our neighbours kept offering me, as he feared it might be polluted. Our water he filtered through his shirt – to trap the silvery dust in it – before storing it in a jerry can. Every morning he would ask me if I needed a drink, and then, as we had no cup, he would tilt the can for me to drink from. When food was scarce, he would forbid me to drink too much water until he had found me something to eat, and after I had eaten some maize, he would only ever allow me one sip. I used to complain, to cry out for my absent mother, but to no avail.

My uncle was also always careful when portioning out the maize. He'd give me a few kernels at a time, saving the rest for later. Often he would go without food himself, so that there would be some left for me the next day. Still, I kept whining about how hungry and thirsty I was. It was only when I was older, and had explored the surrounding countryside myself, and met the local people, that I realised how far my uncle must have walked to find villagers who would still be willing to part with a little maize, and how much effort must have gone into boiling or roasting the kernels for me. And when I saw so many die after eating too much dry maize, or drinking water with that silvery film on it, I understood that my uncle had saved my life.

Every evening, when it was a little cooler, Uncle Atem would take me and my cousins, Dut and Yaac, down to the river. We would go upstream, to avoid the crowds – the swimmers and the sick – and the pollution. I still remember how clear the water was – when you stood in it up to your waist you could see your toes and the silvery dust sparkling like diamonds on the sand below.

"Be careful!" my uncle told Dut and Yaac. "You don't want to disturb the water when you fill the jerry can. It'll cause that silvery stuff to rise."

I remember how he used to wash me, and, back at the camp, cover me with a sack – the only one we had – when he put me to bed.

3

The tractors continued their daily deliveries, but it was not enough to feed everyone in Panyido, and men, women and children continued to die every day, every hour of every day. I remember the hungry and the sick wailing in agony, crying out the names of family members who had been lost in the war, or who had died of starvation in the camp. One old man kept saying that he wished that he had died before the war had started. He begged God to take him away so that he would no longer see others suffering. Later that same day I heard people talking about his death. "He willed it," they said.

The tractors brought no peace to the camp. Day or night you would hear people crying out in pain until they fell asleep or died, and then another would take up the lament. In the middle of the night the dead would be collected so that the next day the bodies could be taken to the forest to be buried in a shallow grave, but despite this the stench of rotting bodies was everywhere.

It was hard for relatives to help the sick. Many were so weak that you tried in vain to understand what they were saying. Starving relatives could only hold the shrivelled hands of the dying and listen to their mumbling. These people understood that the war had caused their suffering, and that they were unlikely to survive. They accepted it.

Then one night something remarkable happened. Above the mournful moans of the dying I suddenly heard the sound of applause. People were clapping their hands and laughing! I saw a dying man rise to his knees to clap his hands, then another.

"What is it all about?" someone asked.

"I don't know," someone else replied. "Where did it start?"

It may have been a story someone told. Perhaps a conversation some neighbours overheard. Whatever it was, that night the camp was a wonderfully joyous place and we all thanked God for letting us share in such happiness.

At noon, three days after this incident, we were amazed to see a truck arriving instead of the tractor. It could carry a much greater load and it returned three times each day. We were still hungry, but no longer starving.

The survivors recovered slowly. The leaders of the different communities now started organising themselves. They would wait for the trucks to come, receive the food and then distribute it to the people – making sure that the ones who were not strong enough to compete for their share also had enough to eat.

Then one day a party of Ethiopian relief workers in two Land Cruisers paid us an unexpected visit. They were visibly shocked at what they saw – the conditions such a large number of people were living in; the hunger and the suffering. But apart from giving the little food they had with them to some particularly hungry-looking individuals there was little they could do that day. They left without comment, but the next day a convoy of seventeen long vehicles came, laden with all kinds of food.

Life was good again! As the first drivers made their way through the throng and found a place to park, people pressed forward to open the containers. There were all kinds of tinned foods and fruit! Mangoes! Even peanuts! But as hundreds of hungry men jumped onto the trucks, the feeble were once again pulled down and some were crushed.

Later, men, women and children who had been starving died

of feasting. Many didn't realise that eating too much after a long period of starvation could result in severe stomach disorders, even death. In addition, eating causes thirst, and in their excitement some disregarded the threat of cholera. Again, it was my uncle who saved me and my cousins. He had often advised us about life in the camp: "God Himself will send us supplies," he used to say, "but we have to be responsible. God helps those who help themselves."

He would even tie me up whenever he had to leave the camp, with strict instructions that my cousins should not allow me to eat anything while he was away. They took their duty seriously and I had to beg very convincingly before they would allow me even a sip of water.

Once there was enough food, the relief workers turned their attention to the question of hygiene. They established three clinics. Spaces were cleared under some big trees and the sick and malnourished who had no one to care for them were carried into the shade. Two containers of food had been reserved for them, and these were now opened. Special cooks were appointed.

At last there was ample food for the sick but, sadly, too few helpers to feed them, or to attend to their other needs. Abandoned, they lay in rows like firewood; the living among the dead. Burials were organised by a division of soldiers whose camp had been set up not far from ours. They would appear every morning, collect the able-bodied men and make them remove and bury the bodies – two men to a body. This was not a task they carried out willingly, but it had to be done, the soldiers insisted, for the sake of hygiene.

The relief workers were doing their best to improve our lot, though none of them stayed in the camp with us. Convoys kept coming. There was maize in abundance. But cholera and other diseases were still taking their toll. A large number of huge white tents were supplied to the clinics, but only a few were ever erected as it was not the rainy season when they were delivered, and the shade of the trees was deemed sufficient protection.

The constant supply of food and the good relations between us and the Ethiopians now enabled the elders to make arrangements for the large number of orphans and children who had become separated from their parents when their villages had been attacked. They decided to separate all unaccompanied children from the rest of the refugees so that they might be protected and cared for until the fortunate among them could be reunited with their families. Adults who had been looking after such children were encouraged to hand them over to the camp elders. They were gathered together under a big tree where they were divided into two groups. The boys, who were in the majority (there were about three thousand of them), were taken to a spot about five minutes' walk from the camp. The five hundred or so girls (the ones that had not been integrated into the community) were accommodated in the centre of the existing camp.

I was lucky. I did not have to join the other boys as I still had my uncle.

4

How was I to know that a military training centre had been established in Ethiopia by the southern Sudanese government? How was I to know that the Sudanese People's Liberation Army had embarked on a campaign to mobilise all able-bodied men? Sudan needed them, the SPLA soldiers said, and it was every man's duty to carry on the struggle. When they had fled to suffer on Ethiopian soil, it had not ended their duty to the fatherland.

Uncle Atem resisted the call to arms, but one day he, with hundreds of other men, simply disappeared. I was unaware of what had happened as my cousins and friends took care of me as they had always done in his absence. "He will be back in the evening," they assured me. But he was not.

Some days later Yaac told me, "Uncle Atem has gone to the military training camp to collect a gun so that he can go back home and look for your mama and papa. Don't be scared. He has left you in my care till he comes back for you."

Yaac did take good care of me – for a month – but so many children had now been abandoned by men returning to war that new arrangements had to be made. A large number of boys like me were gathered together and a second group was formed – the "minors" – consisting of boys between the ages of three and ten.

I had always been a valued member of my uncle's small family, but now I found myself in a herd of young children, feeling utterly forlorn. In fact, there were so many of us that as we were lined up for the walk to the place that would become the minors' camp I couldn't see the beginning or the end of the two lines we formed.

The whole place was filled with the noise of children: some were crying; others were arguing with the elders. It was a five-minute walk from the main camp to the new minors' compound, but the trip took us several hours.

As soon as we had reached the place, an elder said, "Boys, I want you to sit down in groups of ten. We've got something for you to eat."

We could see that there was food – it was in a drum that had been cut in half – but groups of ten? It created great confusion. We couldn't count to ten! Some started crying, struggling to understand. In the end, the men who had accompanied us to our new camp divided us into groups themselves. It then became clear that all of this was part of a strategy to keep us from rushing to help ourselves from the drum. They tore empty sacks into pieces and spread them on the ground. Then ten boys were plucked from the line and told to sit around each piece, which was to serve as a kind of communal plate.

Some boys were unable to eat, although they were hungry. Some were greedy and pushed others away from the food they were supposed to share. The polite boys gaped in astonishment at the manners of the aggressive ones. Unfortunately, there wasn't enough food to satisfy all of us, but the elders did see to it that the youngest and the weakest received their share.

Next came our sleeping arrangements. A sprinkling of enterprising guys had made themselves shorts and shirts from old sacks during their time in the camp, but most of us had nothing at all to wear and no bedclothes. Our minders told us to clear a space before nightfall and to dig hollows to serve as beds. We had nothing sharp to cut the long grass with, so the adults – who had been struggling with us all day – had to break the coarse grass with their hands to clear an area large enough to accommodate all the children.

When darkness caught us, some boys gathered to warm themselves by a huge fire our minders had built, while others were staking out their beds. I cried myself to sleep in the hollow I had scratched out of the hard ground. I was feeling very, very lonely. I didn't know any of the boys I was with, and even though some of them spoke Dinka, like me, their accents were strange to my ear. It was clear, however, that they were as troubled and as restless as I was. In one corner, a child woke up and called for his mother. Another, dreaming, jumped up and ran right over the sleeping bodies of the boys around him. One of our minders appeared and comforted the boy who had cried for his mother, but the rest of us had no one to cling to.

When dawn came there was nothing we could do but resume the task of clearing the bush.

At breakfast time we were instructed to line up. It was pandemonium! Each boy fought for his share of the grain. Strong boys pushed into the line ahead of weaker ones. Those at the head of the queue beat away the hands of the others as they grabbed for food. Some, who had managed to snatch a handful, scurried off, pursued by boys intent on robbing them.

That is how we fought for survival. No one cared about anyone else. How much you got was up to you. We no longer thought of our mothers. There was nothing on our minds but food.

The elders might have made our lives easier in this hostile environment had they enforced some basic rules. Instead, they gave us free rein – at least, initially. There was no adequate container for water, so as soon as the fight for food was over we would start the long trip down to the river. We were forced to. Only the very youngest and weakest of the children received water in the camp. The bigger boys were allowed to stay at the river until nightfall, when it was time to clean the compound. Those who were strong enough would manage to get hold of some kwin (phutu) for supper before bedtime. The rest went to bed on an empty stomach, waiting for morning when there would be some more porridge for breakfast.

Maize was now delivered every week and several venturesome individuals managed to secure the sacks it came in. These were used as blankets, or plates to eat from. The sacks were carefully watched, as an inattentive owner would soon find his gone. Relief workers brought jerry cans to store water in, but we still had no eating utensils.

An increasing number of adults and older boys were finding their way to the military training centre. There were rumours that my cousin Yaac's entire unit was among them. I never saw him again.

The boys now had to take over many tasks from their elders. Teams would be selected each morning to go down to the river to fetch water for cooking and to watch over the young children, who were not allowed to leave the camp unescorted. The strongest, most active boys were made leaders. They would see to it that the others did their chores, and would organise the trips down to the river every morning and afternoon. Lingering on the bank was now forbidden. The leaders were also in charge of hygiene and the demarcation of areas to be used as latrines. The few remaining adults guarded the sickbay and the food distribution area, to prevent sick boys from being robbed of their food.

There was no shelter yet, not a single thatched roof, and it was decided that building a structure was to be our next task. We were handed sickles and sharpened pieces of wood, and instructed to cut the tall grass near the camp. We brought back plenty. Next we were sent to hunt for bush-ropes. The elders, however, soon realised that this job was too demanding for some of the children and announced that the time had come to specialise. The younger boys were assigned the task of lugging water and cleaning the camp. The bigger boys – the ten- to fourteen-year-olds – scoured the forest for ropes. The littlest ones remained under the trees until the workers returned and it was time to eat the maize or sorghum porridge the cooks had prepared.

Our diet never varied. It consisted of maize and sorghum. The aroma and taste never changed either. Diesel. The smell of diesel from the big machine that the cooks used for grinding the maize was present, faintly, in every mouthful.

Before long, we had enough ropes to add to our stack of grass, but we needed poles before we could construct anything. Poles could only be cut by grown men – and all the men had gone to join the army. One day a group of Ethiopians arrived with some poles and offered to help us put up our shelters. But as there were not enough poles for both groups of boys nothing was built, until some newly arrived adults were instructed to cut more poles and build huts for us. In the meantime, to facilitate the distribution of food, the children had been divided into units of five hundred. Each unit was now allocated a long triangular hut with a thatched roof resting on poles. There was just enough space for us all to sleep inside, although on rainy nights only the boys in the middle kept dry.

We had scarcely finished these structures when additional accommodation was required. More and more children like us kept arriving. A third group of boys was formed, with eighteen elders to take care of them. Soon there were seven groups, then eight . . .

My cousin Dut had been placed in my group, but in Unit 6. I was in Unit 1. We rarely saw each other.

5

Two and a half years had now passed since my arrival. We were growing up. We had learned a great deal and boys who had initially stood by helplessly were now working as hard as the others. I had grown strong enough to carry a five-litre jerry can, so every day I ran to the river with the other boys whose duty it was to supply the cooks with water.

Panyido was as hot and dusty as ever. There were patches of white dust and patches of red. You could guess where a visitor came from by the colour of his feet. Ours, in the minors' camp, were white. I remember how we used to make fun of the boys from the surrounding communities who sometimes wandered through the camp on their way to fetch water from the river. These boys were often orphans who lived with families who used them to perform the most unpopular chores. "Slave!" we would taunt them. "What are you doing here?"

"I'm not a slave, I'm a minor like you!" they would reply.

"Liar! Look at your red feet!"

Then something happened that upset our routine. The camp administrators decided to reorganise the groups. In some groups, they argued, such as in Groups 7 and 8, the children were all very young, and unable to take care of themselves. So, first Groups 1 to 4 and then Groups 5 to 8 were brought together, mixed, and then divided up into new groups. At first we were disoriented – boys from our former groups, boys who had been close friends, suddenly disappeared – but, gradually, new friendships were formed.

Dut was back! Dut Mayout, my cousin! The quiet one, the frail one. He was afflicted by some disease which caused him a great deal of pain. I recall his mouth in particular; the encrusted lips which always looked so very red and dry. As there was no proper hospital, he received no treatment, and although I loved him more than anyone else – he was the only relative I had left – there was nothing I could do for him, apart from being his best friend.

The elders next turned their attention to education. We were going to learn the alphabet! A call went out for teachers, anyone who had attended an English school would do. One man came forward, a man called Bol Deng Tach. Some Ethiopians from a nearby village also volunteered, but we could not understand them, so they withdrew again.

We had no exercise books, pens or blackboards. In our unit there were more than five hundred boys and only one teacher.

Bol Deng Tach started to sing in a strong voice: "ABCD . . . EFGH . . . IJKL . . . MNOP . . . QRST . . . UVW . . . XYZ . . . XYZ."

This was fun! We joined in.

Next our teacher selected a small bunch of boys. He wrote the letter A on a medicine carton and taught them to write the letter on the ground. As soon as these boys could copy the letter perfectly, they were told to go to the next group and teach them the same lesson – they had to earn their position as the chosen ones before they could return to our teacher to learn the letter B.

While the first class was practising their Bs, our teacher moved to the second group to check on their progress with A. Once he was satisfied, he sent them off to teach more children, and before long a throng of children could be seen scratching their letters in the sand. However, if he wasn't satisfied a child could quickly be demoted from B to A, while others triumphantly reached C and then D, and eventually XYZ!

Once we had learned the capital letters we started all over again with the small letters, and finally to spell the names of animals, places and objects. Later, some students were given USAID boxes to write on with charcoal. We were given books – in English! Only the boys who really couldn't manage were given other duties, like carving stools for our teachers or collecting firewood.

Being educated meant a great deal to me. I recall a conversation I had with Marco Akec Deng, with whom I shared a blanket:

"Let us always be brothers, you and me," he said.

"Yes. I will be here for you, and you for me," I replied. "Your problems will always be mine."

"And yours, mine."

"I want to be educated," I said.

"Me too, for a good future."

There was lots to do. The camp was improving in many ways. Donors occasionally paid us a visit, and we were taught to welcome them with songs in English: "Welcome, welcome, UNHCR! Welcome, Americans, Congress men!" (Congress men? Concrete men? Whatever. To us it meant "strong men".)

They brought blankets, clothing, cooking utensils and tools. Each boy was given a blanket, a pair of trousers and a shirt. It was an exciting time! Now we could sleep anywhere as long as we carried our blankets with us. Unfortunately, the children who were too young to take care of their belongings promptly lost them, some on the day of distribution. Fighting broke out – "This is my blanket! I left it here when I went to the river!" – and the strong robbed the weak, who in turn waited until lines were forming for food and then grabbed an article belonging to anyone who was not watching. It would be his for a day or two until, in an unguarded moment, he would lose it again.

One day writing materials were delivered. There was now an exercise book and a pencil to be shared between every three boys who were able to write, but having to make do with a third of a book and one third of a pencil was declared an insult by some students, who used it as an excuse to skip school and help with grown-up jobs.

Perhaps it was to take our minds off our missing mothers that the authorities allowed us to participate in the projects that were now underway – the building of more shelters as well as class-rooms – but whatever the reason, when the school term ended we were all given tasks. The older boys were sent to cut down the tall, slender trees that grew in the forest. They were given an axe, but some boys would get impatient waiting for their turn with it and start carving away at the tree trunks with sharp stones. In this way many a tree was felled. We younger boys carried the tree trunks back to camp, where we helped to join the poles together with wild vine and erect the frameworks for the shelters and class-rooms. Then we would flatten bundles of grass and tie them to the poles to form walls and a roof. We did all the work ourselves, except when something was too heavy to carry and teams of grown-ups would assist us.

Military discipline was now maintained. Sixteen grown-ups were put in charge of each group, two per unit. We called them teachers. Units worked together as teams. Leaders were appointed and made responsible for the younger boys. Each morning they would get the boys to line up. Even the littlest ones had to be present. Then the teachers would allocate tasks to those capable of performing them. The children who were too young to work would remain in the compound with the sick. After lunch, we would work in or near the camp, cleaning and tidying. When that was done, we would be allowed a dip in the river before supper and bedtime. The rules were strict, but we had come to understand that they were necessary.

When at last each unit had completed eighteen houses, arranged in a circle around a kitchen, as well as a teachers' house near the storeroom, we were told to build ourselves two classrooms. Units competed feverishly to finish ahead of one another, as the first school to open would receive the pick of the new equipment and materials delivered by the UNHCR. We were kept running all day as by now we had to walk long distances to find suitable grass, and often left at dawn in order to be back before the sun and thirst would affect us too severely. Soon our enthusiasm was waning. Some of us were simply too exhausted to continue working. Boys who performed other jobs refused to fetch water as well. I was part of it all. Lugging jerry cans of water was hard work and the older boys who accompanied us wouldn't let us rest along the way. Instead, they would beat those who were slow or reluctant; they pushed us on until we were too tired to care.

Finally, the school buildings were completed. Visitors expressed their amazement that such fine sleeping quarters and classrooms could have been built by the boys themselves.

When school resumed, we were all put in Grade 1. This time there were exercise books and pencils for all, and we could once again practise our As and Bs. After school we still had chores to do, but we were also allowed to play games like football with balls we made from rags and plastic bags tied together.

In the evenings we would go to bed covered in dust – such was the life of kids who had no mothers to make them go down to the river to wash.

One of the lessons we were taught was a grim one. We were excited when all the boys were ordered to gather in the camp one day. Something important was going to happen. There were SPLA soldiers everywhere; their commanders looking very impressive in their smart uniforms. They had brought loudspeakers and tied them to the branches of trees. We sat in our units, waiting. Then six men were led past us. I was sitting too far back to actually see the firing squad, but I heard the shots. And I heard the gruff voice coming from the loudspeakers: "Let this be a lesson to you!"

Later we learned that two of the men had been executed for stealing guns and ammunition to sell to the bandits. Two others had apparently been accused of raping a mother and daughter in Panyido. They deserved death, we told one another. Until a week later, when a cloud mysteriously appeared – in the middle of the dry season. There was a single flash of lightning. It struck the hut in which the mother and daughter were sheltering. The hut caught fire but the two women survived.

I recall the good times we had too, times I always associate with one boy, Cyer Maror. He was older than me, tall and thin; a funny, sociable boy who, after supper, used to entertain us with jokes and impersonations. He made us laugh at ourselves. His stutter was never seen as a handicap. In fact, it made him rather unique.

Then the market came! Near our camp some Ethiopians had set up stalls – the first we had ever seen and a great temptation to young and old. The boys were soon loitering in every corner, gazing at the food and the great variety of articles for sale or running off with a titbit they had snatched. The traders introduced us to their traditional dish, endjira – a large rice pancake served with a variety of spicy meat and vegetable dishes. You tore off a piece of pancake, gathered up some of the fragrant filling, shaped it into a little bundle and put it into your mouth. The main attraction, however, was the fried maize-meal cakes. They were crisp and tasty, and the traders were willing to exchange them for sickles or axes from the camp, or the blankets, soap, cooking utensils and cooking oil we were regularly issued with. The minors' camp was raided for articles we could barter. It was turned upside down. School was forgotten.

When the teachers realised what was going on they instructed one hundred and fifty boys from each unit to patrol the footpaths leading to the market, and threatened to punish any boy caught near it. I knew this, but one day when I saw a group of older boys returning from the market, chewing what they called alawa-luban (bubble gum) and smoking cigarettes, I could no longer resist the temptation. I managed to sneak past the monitors unnoticed, clutching the bar of soap I had been given for washing my shirt and shorts. An Ethiopian trader saw me crossing the dusty road, grabbed me and pulled me into a gap between two stalls. He took my soap and pressed two silver coins into my hand. I had never seen money before, but I took the coins and ran to the stall opposite his. Before I could explain to the shopkeeper what I wanted, though, the security boys appeared, confiscated my money and took me to a tree where I joined a group of captives who looked as miserable as I felt. And so we returned to the minors' camp – and to the detention centre behind the area occupied by Group 6 – each boy holding on to the shirt of the one ahead.

As punishment we spent a night and day without food before we were all given ten lashes with a stick and released. I never attempted to visit the market again.

6

It was in Panyido that the animists among us – I was one of them – first came into contact with Christianity. Those in the camp who knew about Jesus started sharing their faith with those who did not. There were two denominations: Roman Catholic and Protestant. Each group marked out a chapel under the trees and brought benches for their parishioners to sit on. From the start the Protestants – with their singing – drew the larger number of followers, although the Catholics – who established a clinic to provide for the sick and injured – were also popular.

Prayer soon became an everyday way of speaking to God, of communicating to Him our sorrow and the suffering of our fatherland. Sunday services were well attended, by both those who had already committed to Christianity and those who had not. I chose to attend the Sunday prayers held by the Catholics, but did not join the catechism class.

In 1990 a baptism was organised by the Protestants. When the fateful day arrived a great number of boys gathered under the trees, singing the rousing songs they had been taught in the Dinka language to celebrate the occasion. I could not stay away – I had to go and see.

I was watching from a distance with some others when the boys were lined up under the trees. While the boys who were to be baptised were being organised, prayers were conducted by the pastors. I was fascinated and longed to be part of it. Eventually – the queue was long and moved slowly – I went up to one of the organisers and asked him if I could also be baptised. "I'll have to find out for you," he replied. "These boys have already completed their catechism."

He went off to speak to some higher authority, then returned to announce that, as there wouldn't be another baptism anytime soon, anyone who wished to be baptised that day was welcome to attend the ceremony. We could attend catechism classes afterwards, he told us. I was delighted and quickly joined the line to register.

At last it was my turn. "What's your name?" a man asked me.

"Aher Arop," I said.

"I mean your Christian name. A name like Abraham or Daniel or Jacob."

"Oh, I want to be Santo," I told him.

"No, sorry. Santo isn't a Protestant name," he said, shaking his head. "You can't be Santo."

"If I can't be Santo, I don't want to be baptised," I replied.

"Look, here's a list of names." He read some out to me. "Just choose one of these."

But I was adamant, and, eventually, he relented. "All right, then, you can be *Santino*," he said, writing the name on a small piece of paper so that I would never forget it.

And so it came to pass that I was baptised Santino.

But who was I, actually? Aher – the name my mother had given me – or this new guy, Santino?

A boy I knew started calling "Santino, Santino!" and the others soon followed suit.

Much later, in Kakuma Refugee Camp in Kenya, I was to complete my catechism and be confirmed as a member of the Roman Catholic Church.

7

It was in May 1991 that President Mengistu of Ethiopia was overthrown by rebels from northern Sudan This made it very difficult for Sudanese refugees from the south to stay in Ethiopia as we were now at the mercy of the new Ethiopian government, one that was collaborating with the Sudanese rulers from whose tyranny we had originally fled.

So, when rumours of an imminent attack by government forces reached us, we were left no option but to run back to Sudan. On the night that we heard that fighting had broken out some hours from us, the children were ordered to leave first and to run for the border. We were reassured that the part of Sudan we were heading for was controlled by our own soldiers, the SPLA.

I was in one of the last groups of minors to leave. The road was crowded and it was dark, but the enemy was fast gaining on us, pushing our defenders back, and we had to press on. As we ran we could hear bombs exploding, just like when we had fled Sudan for Ethiopia. Now we were rushing back!

After walking all night and most of the following day, we reached the Gilo River. Little did I know that once we had crossed it, it would take us another night and another day of walking to get to the border town of Pochella.

The river bank was congested with people. The first minors' groups had crossed to the other side, but the earth was parched and there was no food to be found. As most of the refugees had already consumed the little they had carried with them, and there was obviously no food on the other side of the river, some were talking about turning back. We were back in hell, just like in those early days in Panyido. Meanwhile, the level of the river was rising, and soon it was coming down in flood. It seemed impossible for those still on the Ethiopian side to cross it.

Our enemies were on their way to kill us and we were trapped!

That afternoon, when people were still milling around, wondering what to do, the soldiers we had relied on to protect us came running wildly from the front line, their shirts tied around their waists. The enemy had evidently destroyed everything behind us. The SPLA soldiers ordered us to jump into the river and swim for our lives, or, if we were unable to swim, to follow the river to where we would reach Sudanese territory controlled by the SPLA. They would cover us, they promised.

Then I recognised Salva Kiir Mayardit. He was the SPLA commander in charge of refugees, a man who had visited Panyido several times. Here he was, struggling with his own bodyguards, who were trying to drag him to safety. He would not cross the river and leave thousands of refugees to be slaughtered, he shouted, as his bodyguards pulled him towards a boat on the river bank. Commander Salva Kiir looked at the hundreds of youngsters who had gathered near the boat. "Please! Help the children!" he shouted. "They are innocent. Help them!"

He refused to get onto the boat until his bodyguards had tied a large sheet of plastic to it. They then urged some boys to grab hold of it, so that they might be pulled across the water. Commander Kiir then turned to me. "Can you swim, boy?" he wanted to know. "Do you think you can make it across on your own?"

"Yes, sir. I can swim," I said. "I have already been on the other side, but there's no food over there, so I came back before the water rose so high." I told him this because I didn't want him to think I wasn't brave.

He understood. "Well," he said, "let's cross first, and then I'll order my soldiers to go and collect some food for you."

Young boys were swarming towards the river. "Those of you who are able to had better swim," Commander Kiir said to those nearest him. "We'll take your clothes for you."

He then told his bodyguards to help some of the boys onto the boat with him and pull the rest across using the plastic sheet. We who remained on the river bank were overwhelmed with respect for our leader.

It was true that I could swim, I had learned to in the camp, but this river was terrifying – big and powerful! Water was rushing down, splashing up against the rocks. However, Commander Kiir had said that we were to swim, and had offered to take our clothes to the other side and to provide food for us. My heart told me that I could do it. I took off my clothes and handed them to one of the commander's bodyguards. Then, before the boat's engines had even started, I jumped in and swam, making for an island in the middle of the rushing water.

I had almost reached it when the shooting started, sub-machine-gun fire that left me in no doubt that the enemy had arrived. Hundreds, who were unable to swim, threw themselves into the water and drowned. Others were shot and killed. Infants came floating past me. Their mothers must have drowned, I thought, as I fought with the river.

It was on that day that I learned that a newborn child will not sink. I saw the little ones crying as the water swept them away, but there was nothing I could do.

There was a lull in the shooting when I reached the opposite bank and I attempted to grab hold of a branch that reached down to the water. I knew that I would have to climb up the steep bank, but after swimming the river I didn't have the strength for it. I tried and fell back three times. At last I succeeded. Then, dragging myself to my feet, I ran.

"Lie down and roll!" a soldier shouted at me.

I could not. There were too many dead bodies. I bent my back and continued to run, but I didn't get far before the shooting resumed. Bullets were coming from all directions. Our own soldiers were in front of me. "Don't run!" they yelled. "Throw yourself down flat!"

This time I obeyed.

When the firefight had fizzled out someone shouted at me to get up and run towards the SPLA soldiers. One of them grabbed hold of me and pulled me down behind a fallen tree trunk.

In the meantime, many people who had managed to cross the river now used the lull to get up and run for the road. I quickly joined them.

A priest was standing by the roadside. When he saw that I was naked, he picked up a shirt and tossed it to me. But just as I was reaching out to catch it a bullet struck a tree that stood near us, splitting it in half. "Get away from the road!" a soldier shouted, as the priest and I dived down together. "You two are targets!"

The priest and I rolled in different directions.

There was a rubbish dump in the forest on the other side of the Gilo River. We had visited it once, crossing the river to collect some useful items for the camp, but on that day I ran right past it and continued running through the forest for an hour, smashing through the bush.

When at last I thought that I was out of reach of the bullets I sat down with a group of grown-ups. They were trying to determine in which direction the road lay. "It must be near the mountain," one said.

"I'm not returning to that road," replied his companion. "It's too dangerous. They will see us and drop bombs on us."

More people arrived. Some were looking for lost family members. Others, like me, who had no family to worry about, were thinking about where they could find clothes, how to survive the next crisis and how long it would be before the UNHCR would come to our rescue.

At last the elders reached agreement. We would walk in the direction of the mountain, where they thought we would find the road. The road that the bombs were sure to fall on!

By then a great crowd of people had congregated. Some were cooking. Some were anxious to leave because they wanted to reach Pochella that same night. Others were calling out, trying to locate the relatives of babies and young children they had snatched from the bloody river.

I was able to find a shirt and a pair of shorts – a friend of mine from Panyido had managed to hold on to his bag in which he had some spare clothes – and teamed up with boys of my own age that I knew. They had some beans and maize that they had brought from the camp. We cooked, resting in the middle of the crowd, watching people passing by.

When my companions and I had finished our meal we got to our feet and rejoined the dazed throng. We tried to stay together and, for safety, to keep to the middle of the crowd, but we soon got separated. I plodded on until I was too tired to continue, then joined a group of people sleeping on the side of the road. I was unable to sleep, though, so I got up again and kept moving until I found another family sleeping on the side of the road. I huddled up with them as more refugees joined us.

I was still awake when, around midnight, there was a sudden commotion. I couldn't see anything, but I heard people calling out and scrambled for safety in the middle of the group as a voice wailed somewhere in the darkness. Someone had been dragged off by a lion!

When at last morning came we found an ownerless bag lying on the ground and discovered the victim had been a teacher. Some soldiers told us that they had seen the lion, but couldn't shoot for fear of hitting the refugees.

We still had a long way to go, and it was already getting hot, so those who had food found a place in the shade and started cooking breakfast. A few were willing to share what they had with us children.

Later that day we reached the Sudanese town of Pochella, where I found my friends in a state of turmoil. We were desperate to join up with the boys from our groups again, but many had disappeared. There were no adults to call us for food distribution. We were alone.

At about ten o'clock that same evening, while the new arrivals were still settling in, we heard the sound of an aeroplane coming from the direction of Ethiopia.

"It's food! It's the UNHCR!" someone shouted.

But others dived for cover. "Lie down! Lie down!" they cried.

The plane flew over Pochella and disappeared in the direction of the river, then it returned. It had been sent by the north Sudanese government to attack us!

"Don't look up!" a woman near me warned. "From a plane your

eyes look bigger than a river. They will drop a bomb on you. Don't look at it!"

As she was speaking, we heard two bombs exploding on the other side of the border. Then the plane came for us.

We learned later that a large number of refugees had been killed in the first strike. In Pochella more cows than people died because, mercifully, the part of the town that was hit was only sparsely populated.

And that was how President Omar Hassan al-Bashir's government welcomed us back from Panyido.

8

We boys stayed in Pochella for some time. The situation was almost as bad as it had been in those early days at Panyido. However, once again, after a few days the elders took charge and called out group and unit numbers to return us to our original groups. As more gunships were expected, we were then transferred to a part of the forest a ninety-minute walk from the town. In that dense and gloomy place we were to hide from the eyes of the enemy. We were not allowed to spread white shirts on the ground or to pitch tents. Fires were also forbidden. Although we were now safe from attack, we, the survivors of the 1987 famine, were once again starving.

The communities of refugees who had remained at Pochella were no better off. There were masses of people and no supplies. Nor were there any villages nearby where clothes might be exchanged for food. Every kind of leaf and fruit had been tried and what was edible had been eaten. There was nothing left.

This was our second famine and we were well aware of how many had died the first time. My friends, Gor Koal and Kout Deng, and I decided that we would live. One morning we left the minors' camp to pay the communities a visit, but we quickly realised that there was no one there who could assist us. We would have to fend for ourselves.

We had been told that there was a cattle camp somewhere in the dark forest, so the three of us set off in the direction of Ethiopia to look for tracks that might lead us to the cows. We did find spoor and followed it towards the forest, hoping we wouldn't have to go too far, for the forest was a dark and frightening place and all we had with us was one small knife. After a while we stopped to discuss our situation. "Let's follow the tracks for another hour," Gor, the eldest, suggested, "and if we haven't found anything by then, we'll turn back."

I was the youngest, but they knew that I was committed and would enter that dark place where no human voices could be heard, only the calls of birds. Kout also agreed to the plan and we continued on our way, following the cattle trail until we reached a valley where many tall trees grew.

Suddenly we saw something moving in the bush. It was a kind of tawny colour – like a lion! We told ourselves to be brave. "Don't run! Let's see what it is first," Gor said.

We knelt down for a closer look. It had horns! Lions do not have horns, so we took heart and approached it very cautiously. It was a cow – a sick one, but a cow.

But how to kill it so that we might eat it? The problem was our knife. It was very small and blunt. After much discussion, we agreed that the cow was dying anyway so we might as well wait until it was dead. It would provide us with food for many days and we could just stay there and eat and eat. We praised God for the gift of a cow that was near death.

There we sat, in the undergrowth, concealed by the branches of tall trees.

"We are wasting our time. Why don't we just kill the cow?" Kout suggested after an hour or so. By now it was about four o'clock and the forest was fast growing dark.

Gor disagreed. "Suppose the owner comes and accuses us of stealing his cow? We'd better wait."

"It will take too long," I protested.

As we were two against one, Gor agreed to let us try. We approached the cow gingerly, hunger lending us courage, then touched its body to see if it would react. It was indeed very weak, but when we touched it, it suddenly stood up on its four legs and looked at us with wild eyes.

"Okay, let's wait for it to die, as Gor said," I ventured.

But we had scarcely sat down again when the cow started ambling away. We jumped up, but, weak or strong, the cow ran faster than we were able to.

"Let's follow it anyway," Gor said. "Maybe it knows where it has come from, and we can sleep there."

The cow, however, vanished into the darkness of the forest, and we were afraid to follow because it might take us to a place where there were wild animals like lions.

We just stood there, trying to remember how to get back to the camp. Then Kout reminded us that we had been walking since early morning and would never get back before dark. There also might be lions on the way – we could hear them roaring behind us – and we agreed it would be better to walk until we found a sturdy tree to sleep in.

We walked right into three lions!

Gor was two years older than Kout and he immediately took charge. "Don't run," he whispered. "Lions hate cowards. If one sees you acting like a coward he will attack you. We'll be safe if we stay together."

So we pretended to be brave. We kept walking, watching the lions as they disappeared into the bush, then appeared again. We were terrified, but didn't allow ourselves to walk any faster. We even made an attempt to sing, but it didn't sound too good. At last we came to a big tree. They pushed me up first, then followed –

just in time, for a few seconds later a huge lion moved proudly under our tree, stretching himself.

We were trapped. There was nothing we could do. Later, when we heard a gunshot and some cattle lowing, we called as loudly as we could, but no one came to our assistance. We spent the night talking, and sleeping as best we could.

The next morning the lions were gone. "We'd better stay where we are," said Gor. "It's a trick. They will attack us as soon as we climb down. Let's shout again. Maybe someone will hear us."

So we shouted until we heard people approaching, firing their gun. Suppose they walked right past us! We kept shouting until three soldiers appeared.

They were the enemy – bandits who had killed some of our people. Would they shoot us too?

We spoke to them in Arabic and told them what had happened to us. They said the cattle were not far and escorted us part of the way.

It was early morning when we reached the cattle camp. Many other minors had also found their way there, looking for meat. There were five dead cows, and their owners had dragged them away from the live cows to skin them. Each carcass was surrounded by children, watching, waiting to see if they would be given anything. My friends suggested that the three of us should wait at different carcasses, so that if one man did not want to give us a piece of meat, another might.

Gor and Kout were lucky. They each received a share from the first four animals while I was still waiting for the fifth to be skinned. When they came to show me their booty we concluded that Gor should take the meat some distance away and stay with it, while Kout and I waited for more.

The man I was watching explained that he would keep half the meat and divide the other half among the seventy-three minors who were still waiting for a share. There was an atmosphere of eager anticipation.

Then Gor appeared and pandemonium broke out.

When he joined the queue the number of boys increased to seventy-four and the owner of the cow had to reapportion the meat. The boys got impatient and started snatching pieces from the piles.

I was sitting on my haunches, guarding my portion, but someone grabbed it and made off with it. All I could do was to find someone I could rob in return. I saw some boys running off with meat. They were looting someone's share. I joined in. Then I heard Gor shouting and I realised that the meat I was stealing was our own. Kout heard Gor too and threw away the meat he was carrying to rush to Gor's assistance. Gor got hold of a lung, while Kout was chasing a boy who had stolen a large portion of our share.

Soon I found myself fighting a boy my own age over a small piece. He was thin but determined. When the general brawl abated a man appeared and offered to solve our problem by cutting the piece of meat in half. "No!" cried my opponent, and we resumed our struggle. When someone else suggested the same solution a little later, it was I who refused. I heard Kout's voice urging me on: "Come on! If you lose that meat we'll have nothing left!" he said.

"They are the same age. Let them fight until the stronger one wins," someone said.

But we were getting tired and in the end we agreed to let an older man divide the meat between us.

I sat down with my friends, but I was still so angry that I started blaming Gor for not guarding our meat. Accusing him did not make things better, though. We needed to roast our meat and eat. A boy was using a tin he had found to boil some meat in. We liked the idea so we promised him two bits of cooked meat for the use of his tin, and traded one small piece for some salt. By then it was raining, but we were not deterred and soon we were having our meal.

When our hunger had been satisfied, we started wondering what to do next. We might as well return to our camp, we concluded, as the cattle herds were leaving the area. Many of the other boys agreed. They knew the way back, so we tagged along.

9

The situation at the camp did not improve. One day one of the elders offered to go and shoot a monkey for supper. There are people who refuse to eat monkey meat because their faces and hands look so much like a human being's, but the soldiers in the camp did occasionally hunt monkeys. If you found a troop you could kill as many as you wished, they said. But I had once witnessed one being shot and knew that it was anything but easy to shoot a monkey that was begging you not to kill it. In this case, he had hung from a branch, touching his wound. When he had seen his own blood, he had started crying and reaching out to the hunters as if in supplication, showing them the blood on his fingers. "Kill him," a soldier had said. "If we leave him like that, he will only suffer and die anyway."

An elder once told me a story about monkeys that left a lasting impression on me. In a forest, he said, there were so many monkeys that the villagers would steal their babies to play with. One day a gang of boys caught a baby monkey and took it home to be their pet. The mother, who refused to give up her child, furtively followed the boys to the village, where a woman had also given birth to a baby.

When the boys grew bored with their new toy they left it in the house and went to play in a nearby compound. As soon as everything was quiet, the little monkey's mother scurried down, grabbed the human baby – from where its mother had laid it down in the shade of her house while she was going about her chores – and ran up a tree. The human mother saw it and screamed. People came running. The monkey was gently cradling the human child in her arms, but as soon as anyone attempted to climb the tree she made as if to throw it to the ground.

"We'd better ask her nicely, not force her," someone suggested.

So the monkey was asked kindly to bring the baby down. She repeated their gestures, but the villagers didn't understand what she was trying to tell them until the boys returned and confessed to what they had done. Then everyone understood why the monkey had come to the village.

The little monkey was released and it immediately dashed up the tree. The monkey mother received her child and carefully examined its body. Then she nodded in acceptance. She was, however, still afraid to come down, fearing that the people below might kill both herself and her child. But the elders guessed the reason for her reluctance and asked the villagers to disperse, to give the monkey a chance to come down the tree. When they had gone the monkey climbed down very carefully. She gently laid down the human baby, then disappeared up the tree again. The bystanders applauded, realising that monkeys knew something about life. She could experience pain, like human beings. Some were still threatening to kill her, but others guarded her until she and her child had found their way back into the forest.

A starving child, however, will eat anything.

10

In July 1991 the SPLA platoon in our area was ordered to leave and move to the equatorial region of southern Sudan. Many minors were thinking of following the soldiers, rather than starving to death as so many had done in Ethiopia in 1987. We had strict orders not to leave our camp, but I, as an individual taking charge of my own life, was determined to escape.

And I did. My friends Gor and Kout opted to stay, but many of my peers and I furtively followed the platoon through the forest until we judged that if they discovered our presence it would be too late for them to return us to the camp. One by one we joined their ranks, keeping up with them until evening. It was only when they lined up for roll call that they realised how many minors they had in their care – more than seventy. They had no choice but to allow us to travel with them to the next camp, a journey that would take us a fortnight.

I was soon to regret my foolishness. How could I have followed the soldiers when I had no idea where they were going? They weren't carrying any food, but expected to hunt on the way, they said. And they did hunt, for themselves and for us. It was the rainy season, though, and the sodden ground, the frequent showers and the clouds of mosquitoes made life miserable. Often it was too wet to cook, even if the men had managed to kill some animal, and we had no mosquito nets.

Nature can be cruel and some days were pure hell.

"Do you see that mountain?" a soldier asked me one day. We had long since left the forest behind and the mountain loomed ahead;

it was massive, its summit obscured by cloud. "It's called Jabal Jissa: the Mountain of Punishment," he continued. "If you are not brave, you will die before you get to it. But if you take heart and reach the mountain, you can indeed thank God."

That afternoon the soldiers told us that they would go hunting and bring us something to eat, then we would spend a day and a night resting before we attempted to cross the marshy plain between us and the mountain. It would be perilous as there would be nothing to shield us from the eyes of the gangs of murderous bandits that inhabited the area. We would have to move fast.

The trek towards the mountain was indeed hard. We left at dawn, in the rain, and started wading through a swamp. The tall grass made it difficult for us to see where we were going, but nonetheless we trudged all day and night without being allowed to rest. The next morning we stopped under some trees, but it was raining so hard that we couldn't see the mountain that was our goal. We were weak with hunger, but it was too wet to cook, so we just lay down on the waterlogged grass and stayed there until evening came and we could resume our journey. We were drenched and tired and covered in mud. I knew I was supposed to be brave, but it was difficult on an empty stomach. I kept thinking of my mother and my father, wondering where they were and what the use was of struggling on.

The third day started as wet as the previous ones, although it did get a little warmer later. We kept wading miserably through the water until, at around three o'clock, we at last struck dry land. It was there that the soldiers defied their orders. They insisted on taking a rest. Several went hunting and brought back enough meat for all of us.

Soon there was meat on the fire and the men cut some grass for us to sleep on, but I still felt uneasy. The wind had dropped and a huge cloud had engulfed us. There were no proper trees, no shelter, and my heart was heavy. I had not seen a single hut for three days and I knew that this would be no ordinary storm.

It wasn't long before the rain was coming down in torrents. I eventually fell asleep with it beating down on me and only woke when the water I was lying in was so deep that I had to find more grass to build a higher bed. If I could just keep my head above water, I thought, I didn't care about my legs. Others were moving about too, but when the rain stopped at last, we settled down. Gradually our bodies warmed the water around us. We had to lie very still, for if someone turned over, it would cause a little wave of cold water to wake the person next to him. We learned quickly. Stay close to your partner to keep warm and don't move unless he does too.

The next morning everyone was in a hurry to leave the place. We walked all day and night, beating the mosquitoes away and battling drowsiness. It was eerily quiet. The only sound was the *kwik, kwik, kwik* of the mud in the soldiers' boots as we plodded on through the swamp and the *kwuk, kwuk, kwuk* of the bags dangling from their backs. The sky was clear and the landscape was treeless, empty. The great black mountain seemed very near, very intimidating. I didn't know that it would take us a full day to reach it.

That night the moon was full. It hung huge against a deep blue sky. It felt so close. Earlier it had risen spectacularly, but now it seemed not to be moving at all. We would soon leave it behind, I thought – we were moving so fast – but, mysteriously, it stayed above us.

"How many moons are there in Sudan?" I asked a soldier.

"Only one," he said.

"Does that mean that I am looking at the same moon as my mother and father, wherever they are? Are they looking at the same moon right now?"

"Yes," he said and I laughed aloud, thinking that I was sharing a joke with my parents at that moment. The thought gave me courage to deal with my fear throughout that muddy, lonely night.

Before dawn we were met by a horrible stench we could not immediately identify.

"Rotting bodies," a soldier guessed. "A massacre. There are bandits in this area."

He was right. We found the bodies on a patch of flattened grass. They could still be identified by the tribal markings on their faces, although the scavengers had been feasting. There were two women, three children and seven grown men. Some soldiers were dispatched to search the surrounding area, while others buried the bodies. We minors waited some distance away. We were terrified.

"You are lucky we are travelling in the rainy season," one of the soldiers said. "When it's dry this place will show you what war has done to our country. Bandits have killed many people in this area. Their skulls and bones lie under the grass where you can't see them now."

When the bodies had been buried, each soldier took responsibility for one or two children. After seeing what had happened to those poor people I had made up my mind not to cry no matter how hard the soldiers pushed us. When I slipped in the mud I got up quickly and ran to join the line, fearing that the bandits would get me if I fell behind.

At last we reached the mountain. As we made our way onto higher ground I saw some papaya trees and realised that the place must once have been inhabited. But what had become of the villagers?

Later, we slept there, on the foothills of the Mountain of Punishment. The soldiers stood guard all night.

Four days later we arrived at Corchuey, a large displacement camp for southern Sudanese refugees who, like us, had fled the war in Ethiopia. There were some groups of minors too – children that had come from a camp called Dimma in Ethiopia. Approaching the camp, we saw the children first, lining the road, excitedly waiting for the soldiers to arrive. Both soldiers and minors were hoping to recognise faces of family or friends in the crowd. And many did. They could hardly believe that they had found their brothers and sisters. I was hoping to be recognised too, but I didn't expect to recognise anyone myself. I was too young when I was separated from my family – a toddler on my uncle's shoulders. I feared that, even if one of my relatives were present, he or she wouldn't know me because I had grown so tall.

So I just stood there, watching the joy of others as they found long-lost family members or ran up and down the lines to enquire about their parents. I wept when I heard someone being told of the death of a loved one. It hurt me as if I too had lost a parent. There were more boys like me. Some approached me and asked if I had known such or such a person in Panyido. I gave them information when I could and, in turn, explained to people where my tribe used to live and gave them my family's name, but none of the children could help me. There were some elders who claimed that they had known my father before the war broke out, but they couldn't tell me whether my parents were still living in the same village. Others knew my mother's family, but said that none of them was at Corchuey.

Finally, realising that there was no one among the crowd for me, I joined the soldiers under the tall trees.

11

I was seven or eight years old when we arrived at Corchuey. I am sorry I cannot give you my exact age. My uncle had told me that I was born on 30 August, but he was not sure whether it was 30 August 1983 or 1984.

Unfortunately, the conditions at Corchuey were exactly the same as those in the camp we had escaped from near Pochella. The minors, weak like us, were battling to find food – they too had eaten all the edible leaves and the trees were bare. They had been glad to see the soldiers, hoping that they had brought supplies, but were disappointed when it became obvious that they had arrived with nothing more than seventy extra mouths to feed. Like us, some were wondering where the soldiers were heading next. Several were thinking of leaving with them. Others were determined to stay with their new-found relatives.

As for me, having escaped from the camp near Pochella, I was not going to stay in this camp. I left with the soldiers that same evening.

It took us two days to get to Jabal Boma, a military rest camp in the mountains. We were not exactly welcome. They took us for the enemy. On that same day – 18 August 1991 – Commander Reik Machar of the Upper Nile Region had broken away from the SPLA. And here we came marching towards Jabal Boma. Who were we?

Blissfully unaware of these developments, we walked straight into their ambush. But, luckily, we had already passed the test. As we were approaching the camp the soldiers had started singing the "Song of the Movement" – a song every loyal SPLA supporter knew.

"Halt!" cried a military man, who had appeared at the side of the road. We obeyed and he asked who we were and where we were going. We told him. Then he ordered us to follow him in military file and to ignore any familiar faces we might see in the crowd waiting for us. As we entered the camp we saw that there were separate quarters for men, women and minors, but we were marched straight to the parade ground where we were lined up and the minors were separated from the soldiers.

We boys were given five cows to be slaughtered as a welcoming gift, but in our quarters there were a number of other boys who had arrived before us, which meant that we would each receive only a small piece of meat. In the morning we had to gather our own food for a meal – we could pick ourselves some green leaves in the forest, the soldiers at the camp said – which we ate from a communal drum as there were no plates for us.

The soldiers we had come with were now instructed to turn back to the warzone, where Commander Reik had staged his coup. The minors would remain in the military centre till summer, when the roads would be passable and we could be returned to the camps we had escaped from. Bol Madut, the commander in charge of the camp, informed us that planes from Lokichokio in Kenya had started dropping food at Pochella, but I just couldn't face the swamps and the bandits and the Mountain of Punishment again. Going ahead was my goal, not going back.

I stayed at Jabal Boma for three months, until an army convoy of sixteen trucks stopped there en route from Juba to Boma to deliver ammunition to the warzone in the equatorial region. That was exactly where I intended to go – to Kapoeta – and I was determined to be on one of those trucks when they left, with or without permission.

At first, the trucks were taken to a military zone away from the main centre of the camp, but four days later, loaded with supplies, they were back. There was still a little space for people to squeeze in between the cases of ammunition. "Women and the sick first," said Bol Madut, taking charge. "And absolutely no minors."

Hearing this, a number of boys decided to make their way down the road on foot, hoping that a passing truck might stop to pick them up where the commander would not see them. Meanwhile, those lucky enough to be selected by the commander waited in a queue before, one by one, they were let into the enclosure and allowed to get into a truck.

One of the trucks was waiting near the fence. I slipped through and attempted to pull myself up onto one of the huge tyres. Unfortunately, Bol Madut discovered me battling to climb the wheel. He was carrying a long stick and struck my naked back so violently that I fell down, stunned. Then the pain came and I started crying and crawling in the dust. When he saw that I was bleeding he realised he had inflicted a serious injury and ordered a bodyguard to throw me into the truck.

How I hated that man! I didn't care that he was my senior and a commander. I hated him so intensely that if I had had a gun I would have shot him.

By the time I was thrown into the truck it was already moving, and I had to cram my bleeding body into a space occupied by boxes of ammunition and people. I crawled towards two boxes that could support me. A woman had put her legs across one of them and her son was asleep with his head resting on her feet. I stepped over the boy, which caused his mother to jump up furiously, cursing me. "You witch!" she shouted. "How dare you jump over my son!"

Another woman took my part. "You are the witch!" she cried, hitting the boy's mother. "Don't you think that other people's children are human too? Do you think he is a dog? It's the war that has separated him from his mother. Your son is no better than him!"

The mother tried to defend herself, but the more she struggled, the more the women hit her.

I remained silent. I was no longer longing for my mother, because here, in the truck, were women who had expressed my agony for me.

Some hours later we stopped at a place in the desert where the other trucks were waiting. Soon, the officer in charge arrived with the minors who had left Jabal Boma on foot in the hope that one of the trucks would stop to pick them up. There were not too many of them and the soldiers decided to divide them between the trucks.

Later, when we arrived at a distant SPLA outpost, we were relieved to find that the officer in charge of the convoy was an old friend. We had known him when he was a camp manager in Ethiopia and knew that he respected the dignity of minors. He ordered everyone down and explained his plan of action. The women were to travel in the trucks, taking care of the cargo. Then he called the minors to him. He cracked a joke or two and assured us that there would be food enough for us all. We would, however, have to make our way on foot, like the soldiers, because there was just not enough space for everyone in the trucks. Only the sick and the very young were permitted to join the women.

I was included, but my relief didn't last long. There was a deep pothole in the road, filled with water. The driver swerved to avoid it, lost control and crashed into a clump of trees. He braked hard, but by the time the truck stopped I was squashed between a box of ammunition and the strong branch of a tree. I cried for help. Several passengers tried to push the branch away from my back, but were unable to. It was too thick. Then someone had an idea and they removed the boxes of ammunition from beneath me.

That was the last straw! I made up my mind that I would get out and walk. The trucks were moving so slowly that it wouldn't be hard to keep up.

Soon we arrived at a dry area, surrounded by water, an island in a swamp. There were lots of animals, and we knew they wouldn't be able to escape through the water if we hunted them. They provided plenty of meat and it was pleasant to sit there, watching the smoke rising from many fires.

The trucks made several trips from this spot to the outpost at Kapoeta and back again to collect passengers and meat. The truck I was on dropped us at the Kapoeta army barracks and we spent the night in the open veld.

After breakfast the next morning the camp authorities addressed us minors. They told us about the bomb shelters that had been dug and that we were to be on the lookout for gunships, as Kapoeta was a favourite target of the Arab government.

In spite of their warnings, we were not prepared when, on our second day, an Antonov approached soundlessly. We would not have been aware of it at all if we had not seen people running.

"What's going on?" we asked.

"Run for the tunnel! An Antonov is coming!" someone shouted.

I dived into a tunnel and crouched there, listening to the whooing of the bombs dropping. Most were directed at the market and villagers who had not taken shelter in a tunnel in time were now rushing for the entrances. One man was running across a football field when a piece of shrapnel took his head off. It was eerie to see a headless body running till it bumped into a tree.

The plane circled the market one last time, dropped two bombs and then disappeared. Later, in the market, human flesh could barely be distinguished from the meat the farmers had brought to sell.

We minors had no option but to remain at Kapoeta, as this was where the food was. If there were bombings too, well, it was just too bad. But after another bombardment, which lasted for two days, the SPLA transferred us to Narus, a town near the Kenyan border, about a day's drive from the outpost. This time they promised to see to it that we had enough to eat.

Back to school! I was put in Grade 2. There were not many of us, but by Christmas there were rumours that large groups of minors were on their way to join us. It was not until the beginning of April 1992, however, that the first ones – the sick and the bandaged – were brought in by the International Red Cross. And not until later that month that I was reunited with some of my friends from Panyido.

It was from one of them that I heard what had happened to Dut Mayout, my cousin, whom I had last seen in Panyido. One of the new arrivals was Machar, a boy who remembered that I was related to Dut. The news he brought me was disturbing. Dut had made it to Pochella, but when the town was attacked by Arab militia from the north he had been too weak to flee with the other boys. For two days the SPLA soldiers fought desperately, but they were eventually overpowered and the Arabs entered the town. When, some days later, the SPLA soldiers returned and recaptured

Pochella they came upon a burned-out hut and inside the charred bodies of a number of boys, Dut among them.

Later, we all went out together to cut trees for poles to support the plastic sheeting that had been distributed due to the rainy weather. Within a week we were a close community, but the government forces from Khartoum were advancing again. On 25 April they attacked Kapoeta and took it from the SPLA. Then the planes headed for Narus. It was three o'clock that afternoon when we were told to run for the Kenyan border. The enemy was coming!

Carrying blankets and containers of water we ran, sleeping only when we were too tired to continue and could join others sleeping along the side of the road. Only, this time, I forgot that I was fleeing and was still fast asleep when the last of my companions left. I awoke alone.

The men who woke me were in uniform – an unfamiliar uniform I could not identify. The rifles they carried looked very much like the long-barrelled gem of the Arab militias – not at all like the Kalin-shekop AK-47s our own soldiers used. They addressed me in a strange language.

I started shaking.

I was too terrified to speak until they called a Sudanese refugee who could speak English to explain to me that they were Kenyans who had come to help us. I had nothing to be afraid of. "Be brave," they said. "Keep straight on until you get to the Kenyan border. You will find the others there."

Many refugees had indeed congregated on the border, waiting to cross to Lokichokio. The International Red Cross was there too. I joined a group of minors who were lining up for food. It was nice to be fed, but inwardly I was seething. Why had no one woken me? Why had they just left me by the roadside?

I remembered a story a teacher had once told me – a story about a fox with bad manners. The fox would relieve himself just anywhere, not caring about the mess he left or who saw it. The other animals and the people who passed along the path were shocked. They knew who the culprit was, but no one spoke to Fox about it, until one day when Hare asked him, "Fox, what is wrong with you? Why do we always find your droppings under the trees and in the path? Everyone knows they are yours! Aren't you ashamed of yourself?"

Fox was surprised. "Do you know, I have never had a brother or friends to tell me what is good and what is bad," he told Hare. "I thought it was all right to leave my waste along the road. I'm afraid it has now become a habit. I don't think I can change."

My life was like Fox's, I thought. Why hadn't anyone woken me? Why did they just leave me there? Like Fox, I didn't have a brother or a friend.

12

We spent some months at Lokichokio before we were transferred to a camp called Kakuma, a large area not far from the border that had been set aside for the displaced by the Kenyan government and the UNHCR. The camp was situated on arid land, sparsely dotted with abandoned Turkana huts, stunted trees and shrubs. A line of hills in the middle distance marked the border between Sudan and Kenya. We erected some shelters for ourselves using the plastic sheeting and poles the authorities had provided – the sheeting was white with the letters UNHCR written on it in blue.

Soon we resumed our studies under the acacia trees growing along a dry river bed, and in 1993 we moved into the new classrooms the UNHCR had built for us. By then Kakuma was a huge camp and the UNHCR was busy building nineteen primary schools as well as a library. There were enough Kenyan teachers, materials and textbooks for all of us and we were determined to do our very best. A few of the boys battled to keep up, but most of us obtained our Kenya Certificate of Primary Education in 1994. A joyous achievement that was followed only by boredom. Suddenly we had nothing to do but ponder our future which, we were convinced, did not lie in Kakuma. We grew restless. Some suggested looking for a high school elsewhere, others suggested looking for their parents, but to survive outside the camp one needed money. We had no money, but each group of boys did receive monthly food rations – flour, oil and occasionally raw maize or cow beans. We ate very little and sold the rest. Soon we were weak from lack of nutrition, but the coins in our pockets consoled us. We wanted an education. We needed books. And as we had no parents to provide either we would pay our own way.

As Christmas approached, I made up my mind to return to Sudan to look for my mother and father, even if it meant recrossing the warzone. But talk of renewed fighting in the equatorial region of southern Sudan forced me to reconsider. There was no way I would be able to get to the Bahr el Ghazal region, where I thought my parents would be.

Then we got word that at a camp called Ifo, in northeastern Kenya, applications for resettlement in America were being processed. Although the camp had been established for Somali refugees, we were told many Sudanese youngsters were being given the same opportunity. I counted my coins, got onto a bus and headed for Nairobi.

Nairobi! I thought Nairobi was another country near Kenya. In one of our textbooks, *New Friend, Book 3*, there had been an entire chapter on it. According to this book, the people of Nairobi built one house on top of another, as many as a hundred houses stacked together! And there were things they called trains, running to Mombasa harbour. A topic that had always fascinated us was Nairobi's traffic. Our book had told us that in Nairobi people weren't killed by bandits or disease, they were killed in road accidents. But you would be safe if you remembered the rule of the traffic lights: red meant danger, amber was a warning and green meant you could cross the road. There had also been a picture of the traffic in Nairobi in the book and we had understood what it was all about. But telephones? And faxes? And so many houses on top of each other? And a train moving through the mountains? For us youngsters this had seemed a strange world.

If only I could see Nairobi, I thought, America could wait. I travelled all night until, in the morning, we reached Ketali. It was here that I saw my first stack of houses, with people cleaning the windows. It was rather disappointing. The houses were no taller than the trees.

The next stop was Eldoret, where the buildings were much taller and the streets busier. As I had run out of money I had to get off the bus. I wandered about, gazing at the buildings, the traffic signs and the cars. There were so many cars, much smaller than the trucks we knew and of so many different designs. The book had not prepared me for that.

In Eldoret I met a Sudanese family who took me home with them and put me up for a week. Then they persuaded me to return to Kakuma, offering to pay my bus fare. It was not true that there was a resettlement plan at Ifo, they told me, and I would never be able to take care of myself there. I was too young.

So on Christmas Day 1994 I followed them meekly down to the bus station. I felt sad, disillusioned that these people were now urging me to leave. I knew that their own children would be going to Ifo to apply for resettlement, in spite of what they had told me. Nevertheless, I thanked them for their hospitality and boarded the bus for Kakuma.

More cash was what I needed if I was to present myself to the resettlement officers. I ran up and down, selling my rations of flour and oil, until – on 20 April 1995 – I again left the camp. This time I did reach Nairobi. I did see the tall buildings and spent one night there before I caught another bus and headed for Ifo. When I arrived two days later I found that the Joint Voluntary Agency had concluded its programme, and the seven of us, who had travelled together, were too late. All the other applicants had been successful and were waiting for their flights to the United States.

Before I continue my story, I would like to explain to you what I have learned about society. There are different kinds of people. I have come to understand that your character is shaped by your upbringing. If (whether you are an orphan or not) you are raised by someone to whom goodness is important, you will grow up to be good. But if you are left in the care of the wrong kind of guardian, he or she may ruin both your character and your future. It is also true that jealousy destroys. If you live with a guardian who has children of his own, and you are more talented than they are, chances are that he will attempt to ruin your good reputation by saying only negative things about you, while praising his own offspring in the company of others. I have also discovered that some adults to whom orphans are entrusted will take advantage of them and deny them their basic human rights, knowing that there is no one to defend them.

We minors, who spent our childhood as orphans in a war-torn country, have been deprived of a proper upbringing, and have experienced the crushing of our talents. But we have also known kind people, people who valued human dignity, mature adults who understood that a killer will always be haunted by his deeds, but if you help those in need your goodness will be rewarded.

We faced so many troubles at Ifo, but there was one blessing – the ration cards I was able to buy from the boys departing for America They needed money for their trip to Nairobi and we who remained behind could certainly do with some extra food.

There was more good news. The authorities told the seven of us who had arrived too late to be resettled that all was not lost. The Joint Voluntary Agency would be back on 10 October.

Our community grew rapidly and soon the fifty ration cards we had could no longer feed us all. July was a particularly lean month and the UNHCR had to begin negotiations with the religious and political leaders in the camp to find a solution to the food-distribution problems. The Sudanese community was not represented, however, and the leaders of the other communities undermined the authorities' efforts to be fair. It had been agreed that the Sudanese would receive more ration cards in August, but now the date was put back and the cards we did have were confiscated by the UNHCR. We were left to survive as best we could.

The Somalis, who were in the majority, were better off, and those of us who had money or clothes to sell were able to obtain some food for ourselves and our companions from them.

Somehow we kept going until 10 October. Then it was announced that this time resettlement would be for Somalis only. Tough luck. We had no more clothes to sell and the boys whose relatives in Nairobi had supported them while they were waiting for resettlement had to return to their families in the city. I had nowhere to go, except back to Kakuma, and that would cost money.

My friends and I now approached the Somalis, begging for piecework, selling our strength to them, building their brick and corrugated-iron houses or digging their latrines, making life better for them. The Somalis were Muslim, we were Christian, and religious differences fuelled hatred between our communities. Even so, they were our only hope of employment. We were the beggars and we had to swallow our frustration and pride and submit to them.

When 1996 arrived we were still alive, still struggling. I was lucky enough to have befriended a policeman called Kamau – the UNHCR had put Kenyan policemen in the camp for security reasons – and although it wasn't his job, he saw to it that I had something to eat every day. And when I wasn't allowed to visit him in his quarters, he would come to visit me in the Sudanese community. It was only when he was transferred that I returned to a life of deprivation.

There was a time when my friends and I were so weak that we couldn't rise from a sitting position without being overcome by dizziness. I remember the blurred vision, the black spots running before my eyes when I stood up. I would have to wait for the spots to disappear before attempting to walk. Some of us could no longer get up without falling. Several became temporarily blind and had to be led. When we had a little money, we would buy some cow beans, but they were not very nutritious. For more than a year we had no other food.

Come 1997 there were still no ration cards for the Sudanese community and no resettlement plans. We had become accustomed to the humiliation the Somalis subjected us to, but at fourteen I was still considered too young to work – the Somalis wouldn't even let me wash their clothes – though occasionally someone would take pity on my friend Chol Biem and me and offer us something to eat before they sent us back to our own community. But it was money I needed if ever I was to get back to Kakuma.

I had met Chol in Ifo. He was my age, but shorter. He had the confident air of a boy whose parents were around, although, of course, they weren't. "Hey, man, don't worry. Just keep struggling," was his favourite saying.

One morning Chol and I tried the Ethiopian community. We found a man mending his fence. "Can we help you, sir?" we begged.

"I'm sorry," he said. "You're kids. This is a man's job." We must have looked particularly pathetic, for he added, "But I'll get you a bite to eat. You don't have to work for it."

We started negotiating with him, but he just laughed. "You can't do this work. Why do you insist?" he asked. "All right, I'll tell you what, you can mend one metre of the fence while I get lunch for you." He looked at us rather doubtfully and added, "I'll do the top bit where you can't reach."

This was our chance! We tackled the job with all the enthusiasm we could muster. Chol even lifted me onto his shoulders to reach the spots the man had said were too high for us, and when he returned the man found that we had completed our work and part of his. "Hey, boys, but you're fine workers!" he exclaimed, surprised. "Well done! What was I thinking? Look at the great job you have done! Thank you."

He handed us our lunch and when we had finished eating he paid us 300 Kenyan shillings! That was as much as a grown man could earn in a week, working morning to evening. And then he asked us to come back the next day. "I need help around my house," he said.

We were proud. And excited. All the way back to our community we were making plans, discussing how we would repay the people who had helped us. There were fifty-nine boys in our group and we always shared whatever we had. We agreed that we would give each one a share. We greeted them with broad smiles, wanting to see smiles on their faces too. Instead, they were suspicious. "What have you done? Have you stolen from the Ethiopians?" they asked.

Soon, however, everyone was laughing, convinced of our innocence and their good luck.

We kept our promise to Gheto, our Ethiopian friend. We returned the next day and helped him with odd jobs in his compound. He left to attend church after a while, but Chol and I spent the entire day eating and working and earning good money. We were soon given a permanent job – fetching water in a wheel-barrow for his church – for which we were paid 1 200 Kenyan shillings a month.

We were now well equipped to weather the long wait for re-settlement. People came to know of our reputation and called on us to do small jobs for them. And although we were supposed to be at school, not at work, it was great to be earning money. We continued to share some of it with our community – many of our friends wanted to return to Kakuma and asked for contributions, and we also had to continue buying food for all of us – but Chol and I also managed to save some money. A big Ethiopian gentle-man acted as our bank. And after a while I had 7 000 shillings in my account and Chol had 9 000.

Gheto soon invited us to bring more boys to work at the church. When he left for Nairobi on business, I was put in charge of his house and his forty-eight ration cards. Then the UNHCR gave Chol a job distributing oil and flour to Somali refugees. Twice a month rations were distributed to the refugees in Ifo and certain lucky individuals were given the job of distribution. Suddenly, Chol was one of these people. This presented a great opportunity. My friends and I would queue up at Chol's gate with our forty-eight ration cards and Chol and his colleagues from the UNHCR would not skimp.

However, despite all of this, I had not given up my wish to be educated. It was my hope for the future. Collecting rations twice a month and doing odd jobs did not have to keep me away from school, so I enrolled at a Somali high school. Many Sudanese elders encouraged me and promised to support me. "We want you to ful-fil your dream," one of them said. "I can see that your plans are good. We have always known you as someone with ideas and we know that you will find ways to survive, even while you are attending school. Go for it! God will help you."

But while I was better off, conditions had not improved for the Sudanese community. We were still being denied ration cards by the authorities and security in the camp had also not improved. A Somali fired shots at us one night, killing one and wounding many, but there was little that we could do as we were in the minority. They also continued, however, to be a source of income and many Sudanese refugees swallowed their pride and did whatever the Somalis wanted done. Others went out to collect firewood to sell to them. This was a dangerous pursuit as there were gangs of bandits in the vicinity who would taunt the boys over their lack of tribal markings and then pretend to put the matter right by nicking their ears and faces with sharp knives.

I was in the bush myself, once, collecting firewood with twelve others, when we were confronted by three armed Somali bandits. "Drop your wood! Sit down! Sit!" they ordered.

We obeyed. They inspected our clothes and belts and took what they liked. As they were about to release us, one unexpectedly hit me with a stick for no apparent reason – I had certainly not provoked him. Both my friends and the other bandits were taken aback. One of the bandits addressed me: "Have you ever met this man?"

"No," I said.

He then turned the question back on the bully who had struck me. He also said that he did not know me. "Then why are you beating him? Leave him alone," the bandit said. In the end his companions had to use force to restrain him.

Back at the camp, the other youngsters made fun of me. "Why

does he hate you so much? How could you not have met him before? Have you quarrelled?"

That's life, I suppose. There will always be people who need someone to hate.

13

The thought of settling in America no longer occupied the minds of the Sudanese community at Ifo. Our immediate concern was always with food. With the Somali Muslims living next door the Sudanese women were not allowed to show themselves outside our area, so the women and their children used to set traps for doves inside the camp wherever there was not too much traffic. The few birds they caught provided much-needed protein. Well, the UNHCR might have forsaken us, but God did not. In January 1997, after a particularly dismal Christmas, the nets were spread as usual over the water that was used to lure the birds. Quite unexpectedly an enormous swarm of strange birds – a species that none of us, not even the grown-ups, had ever seen before – descended from the sky and flew straight into the nets. There were so many that for a moment we just stood there gazing at them. Then everyone rushed at once to collect the birds that were floundering helplessly in the water. The birds repeated the performance four times, then finally flew away. There was more meat than we could ever possibly eat. But was it safe to eat these foreign-looking birds? Someone would have to test the meat. "Take one, if you want to try," someone offered.

Little children jumped at the chance. A few birds were roasted and the aroma of the cooking meat was just delicious. I cautiously took a bite. These birds tasted even better than the doves we sometimes caught!

The question everyone asked was: Would they be back? The nets were prepared once again and, promptly, at eight the next morning, the birds came swooping down. There were even more than the day before. Excited men, women and children were running about, collecting food – the adults had postponed their chores to join the children. That evening even larger nets were prepared. And the birds kept coming, providing food for every member of the Sudanese community.

On the fourth day, deputations started arriving from the UNHCR and the various communities. They came to witness the sight. They studied our technique carefully and some, like the Ugandans, made their own nets and spread them over sheets of water in their own areas. The following morning our nets were once again swarming with floundering birds, but none of the other communities caught a single one.

Every day they would swoop down on us and only on us. The excitement would last for an hour and then they would be gone. After each episode a number of birds would remain pecking on the ground, watching us spread the nets once more, seemingly unconcerned. Then the swarm would return again and again – always five times. After the fifth harvest we knew we could pack up and go home. We had more than we could possibly eat and the UNHCR officials and refugees from other communities were queuing up to buy from us – at three Kenyan shillings a bird! We also dried some meat for future use. The Sudanese were no longer desperate for food and none of us had to dig a Somali toilet ever again.

Around this time the authorities concluded their negotiations and announced that from 10 October 1997 the Sudanese refugees would also receive ration cards for food, blankets, cooking pots, plates and other treasures. Meanwhile, we continued to gather our daily supply of birds, until the morning of the ninth.

On the tenth the birds were gone!

We all understood that God had provided for us for as long as we needed Him to. We spent the day receiving and organising supplies, but that evening some members of our community prepared their nets again. We were all curious to see what would happen in the morning.

"They won't come. God will not send them again now that the UNHCR is helping us," someone said.

"Don't you dare catch any if they do return. I will help them escape!" another threatened.

"Let us just let them drink in peace tomorrow. We owe them some gratitude for having fed us for nine months," a third voice added.

They never returned.

The Sudanese community spent that Sunday in thanksgiving and celebration. We were awed and overjoyed when we realised that God was on our side, that He had provided for us. This thought meant more than the food we had eaten.

There is a passage from the Bible that I have memorised: "Jesus said to his disciples, 'Therefore I tell you, do not be anxious about your life, what you shall eat, nor about your body, what you should put on, for life is more than food, and the body more than clothing. Consider the ravens: they neither sow nor reap, they neither have storehouses nor barns, and yet God feeds them. Of how much more value are you than the birds. Which of you being anxious can add a cubit to the span of his life?'" (Luke 12:22–25).

Years later I was told that the birds were sandgrouse from Botswana, but I have never seen a single one since, not anywhere.

14

Life was getting better. I was taking care of some of Gheto's ration cards – he had given me four of the forty-eight he possessed – which meant that at every distribution I received lots of nice things. I was also attending school and had reached Form III, halfway through high school. I was even taking extra courses in agriculture, woodwork and joinery.

When my two-year woodwork and joinery course finished at the end of 1997, I made up my mind to spend the little money I had saved on a trip to Nairobi where I hoped to find a sponsor – as a number of my friends had done – and finish high school. Even if no one sponsored me, I reasoned, I did have 7 000 Kenyan shillings and could pay my own way. The Kenyan officials, however, shattered that dream. They kept extorting bribes from me all the way to Nairobi and I was relieved to reach the city with any cash at all.

Luckily, on the bus I ran into some old friends from Ifo who put me up in Nairobi for four days. Among them was William Agar. I had hoped for some support from the church, but didn't know how to approach them. To Agar I mentioned the possibility of trying my luck in Uganda, but he had been to Kampala and told me that my chances of getting the UN, an NGO or a church to sponsor me were slim. He suggested Dar es Salaam in Tanzania instead. On 5 March 1998 Agar accompanied me to the bus station and I bought a ticket.

The bus arrived at five o'clock and I boarded. Once again I was travelling to a destination I had never been to and where I knew no one. I had done so many times before, but this time I was completely alone. There were no minors on the bus, no one who shared my experiences, but once again I hoped to survive without parents to consult or a guardian to take care of me.

A Tanzanian girl had the seat next to mine. She was tall, slender and of a dark complexion. It didn't take me long to say "Hi".

"Hi," she replied with a smile, "I'm Janet."

Soon we were chatting like old friends. She wanted to know why I was travelling alone and whether I knew anyone in Dar es Salaam. I told her about my quest for an education.

"If you really want to go to school, why don't you go to South Africa?" she said. "That's where the good schools are."

"Money is the problem," I told her. However, I was tempted.

We arrived in Dar es Salaam at noon. It was a hot, hot day, and shirtless street vendors were selling bottled water to perspiring customers. Janet invited me to stay over at her parents' house, but the road beckoned. "Which country comes next, after Tanzania?" I asked her.

"Malawi, or Mozambique, but there is no direct bus from Dar es Salaam to Mozambique."

Janet took me to the bus station and showed me where the bus for Karonga, in Malawi, would stop. I bought a ticket and changed some money into kwachas to pay for my ticket to Lilongwe, which left me with fifty US dollars. The bus arrived early and the driver was kind enough to allow me to spend the night on it.

* * *

Early the next morning I was awakened by passengers gathering outside and boarding. A man came up to me. "You don't look like the others," he said in Arabic. "Where are you from?"

"Sudan," I replied.

"Salaam alek," he greeted me in Arabic.

"Alekum ku salaam," I replied.

He was so happy to hear Arabic being spoken that he asked the passenger who was sitting next to me to swap seats with him. "I am from Bangladesh," he told me. "These Africans don't understand my English. Perhaps you will be able to help me."

We ended up helping each other. We shared lunch and he talked to me about my life.

"Why are you travelling alone?" he wanted to know. "Aren't you too young?"

I explained my situation to him in detail and when he realised that I was fairly fluent in English he dug in his bag and produced a book. It was by David Schwartz. "Look at the title," he said. "*The Magic of Thinking Big*. You are thinking big, travelling all by yourself in pursuit of your dream. Would you like to read it?"

"Of course I would," I replied.

"Unfortunately, it's my only copy," he said, "and I don't want to lose it. But why don't you read it on the bus, then we can discuss it."

That book was incredible! It was all about my problems. There was a paragraph that I memorised (and I quote as I remember it): "Build confidence and destroy fear in whatever you think to do, whether bad or good, and whatever you have committed to attempt, never turn back before you have found the goodness or badness of it".

It dealt with fascinating topics. One should not be a fool and embark on a journey without having budgeted for it, the author warned, lest one should have to beg fellow travellers for assistance and be ashamed to do so. My heart sank. What was I doing! I was greatly relieved when he continued: "But don't be afraid to ask for help if you really need it. Someone may help you today and tomorrow he may be the one to need help and you the one to help."

* * *

Two days later we approached the border with Malawi. The conductor informed us that the bus would drop us some five kilometres from the border, at a place where there would be bicycles for hire. We could cross the border by bike.

Later, as we were looking at the bikes we struck up a conversation with a man from the Democratic Republic of Congo. Like us, he was on his way to southern Africa. We formed a partnership with him – it would be better to travel together – and he generously offered to pay for four bikes – one for each of us and one to take our luggage.

It was only when we reached the border with Malawi that I discovered that I was supposed to have a passport. A Tanzanian immigration officer called us into a room. He thought at first that I was with the man from the DRC and was surprised to learn that I had travelled, unaccompanied, all the way from Sudan. When my friends explained the situation in Sudan to him, he nodded. "The Malawians will deport you if they find out you are from Sudan," he said. "They have an agreement with the Sudanese government to return people like you to Khartoum. But . . . do you see that footpath? Follow it down to the river until you meet some men. They will help you cross. Your friends can wait for you at the bus station on the other side."

It was drizzling and fine drops were collecting on the tall grass along the path and on the branches of the trees as I made my way down to the river. After a while I encountered two men. They asked me a question I did not understand, then grabbed me and searched me. One found my 50 US dollars while the other took my shirt and shoes.

"What are you doing?" I protested.

"Stop whining! I'll kill you and throw your body into the river!" said one.

I was not afraid of death. I had seen too many dead bodies; dying, to me, was just something people did. I must have looked rather taken aback, though, for the second man took pity on me. He had seen me with my two friends and reminded me that they were waiting for me at the bus station. He accompanied me across the border and took me to them.

There was no need to tell my friends anything. They saw my bare feet and back, and knew. One had a spare pair of slippers in his bag and the other handed me a spare shirt. My Bangladeshi friend paid my fare to Karonga and then they both contributed towards my ticket to Mzuzu. When we arrived at Mzuzu, one bought food for all three of us and the other paid for our accommodation in a guesthouse. And that was how it would continue. They had taken my plight to heart.

When we got to Lilongwe they left me at the station with their bags and went to look for the nicest accommodation they could afford. They returned with three keys – I was to have a room to myself – and a porter. At the guesthouse they suggested that we have a shower and a proper meal and turn in early. I had my own shower, in my own bathroom. As I was drying myself, there was a knock at the door. I couldn't believe it! My incredible companions had bought me a pair of shoes, a pair of trousers and a shirt. How good it felt to be putting on such fine clothes, with my friends waiting for me. Even the shoes were a perfect fit. I showered them with a thousand words of appreciation: "Thank you, thank you so much, my friends!"

Graciously accepting my gratitude they rose and led the way to the dining room. I wondered what the other guests were thinking of the three of us, smartly dressed, smiling and talking like a family – the Bangladeshi was fair-skinned, my Congolese companion was brown and I was black.

The waiters were curious. "Where are you from?" they wanted to know. "You seem to be such good friends. What is it that ties you together?"

We were indeed best friends. We thanked God and ate our meal happily.

15

My two companions were both bound for Mozambique. "If he comes with us we could take him to the UNHCR offices in Maputo," I overheard my friend from Bangladesh saying the next morning. "They will provide food and accommodation for him."

"We can't let him go to a refugee camp in Mozambique," the man from the DRC replied. "The country is too poor. Life in a camp there will be miserable. He'd be better off trying Zimbabwe. Let's rather pay his bus fare to Harare."

"But can we let him travel alone?" the Bangladeshi asked.

"He's already come a long way on his own and Zimbabwe is a better place for him."

"All right."

So we all went down to the bus station. The ticket clerk told us that the bus for Harare had left the day before and that the next one was only due in three days. "Why don't you go to Blantyre instead?" he suggested. "And from there continue to Harare."

So we returned to our guesthouse to think it over. Finally, it was decided that I would accompany them as far as Blantyre the following day. From there they would go on to Maputo, while I would board a bus that would take me through a corner of Mozambique to Harare.

* * *

The following day we reached Blantyre at noon. My friends' bus for Maputo was due to leave at six that evening; mine, for Harare, at six the next morning. In a final act of generosity they gave me ample money to pay for a night's accommodation, a ticket and food.

These two men had given me so much, but I could only thank them again for the kindness they had shown me on that long trip from Nairobi. A trip I had foolishly undertaken without enough money to see me through.

After we had said our goodbyes I went to the bus station to buy my own ticket.

"Where is your passport, boy?" the clerk demanded as soon as I reached the counter. "Who is accompanying you?"

I tried to explain, but he wouldn't listen. I tried harder, but he wasn't interested. "Our buses do not carry illegal aliens like you," he said. "Go away. Unless you have a passport there's nothing I can do for you."

I raced back to where I had left my friends. They were still there. "Hello, friend. You're back! Have you bought your ticket?" they asked.

"No. The clerk refuses to sell me one," I told them. "He says he can't if I don't have a passport."

They went with me to talk to the clerk, but he remained adamant. Eventually, we tried the manager, who was more accommodating. "All right," he said, "you can have your ticket, but only on condition that you promise to report to immigration when you get to the border."

I promised, was sold a ticket, and went with my friends to wait for their bus, which soon arrived. I stood there waving and waving until they disappeared in the distance.

* * *

Before six the next morning I was back at the bus station and waiting to board the bus to Zimbabwe. Passengers were lining up to show the conductor their passports and their money. The manager who had sold me a ticket was nowhere to be seen, so I waited until last. I had no passport and didn't want to show anyone the little money I had left. But I did have a ticket.

I approached the conductor tentatively.

"No!" he exploded. "Where did you get this ticket from? Please don't waste my time. Go back to wherever you bought this ticket. I can't allow you on this bus."

There was no one I could appeal to. I ran to the manager's office, but he wasn't in, it was too early, and by the time I had swallowed my tears the bus was gone. So I just sat there, wondering how I would survive in Malawi, pondering life in general.

Then I heard a voice. "Hey, young man. Didn't they allow you on the bus?" It was the manager. "Get in the car."

The bus was at a petrol station, just down the road, filling up. The manager called the driver and the conductor and explained my situation to them. Finally, they allowed me to board.

"I need sixty kwacha from you, for the Mozambican police," the conductor said once I had found a seat and the bus had begun to move. "That's their fee per passenger."

I counted my money, but it didn't come to sixty kwacha. So, instead, the conductor gave me two immigration forms to complete, one for leaving Malawi and one for entering Mozambique. "When we reach the border, you come with me to the immigration office, okay?" he said.

I nodded.

By now, my fellow passengers had become interested in me. "Where do you come from, boy?" one enquired.

"From Sudan."

"Where is your mother? Don't you have parents?" another passenger asked.

I told them how the war had split up our family and that I had no idea where my parents were.

"Shame! What did you eat yesterday?" someone else asked.

So many passengers wanted to talk to me that I had to keep changing seats until we reached the border and the conductor called me to accompany him to the immigration office. "There is no need for you to do that!" a mama objected, but the conductor was determined.

He made me wait under a tree while he made his way to the office. I could see him pointing at me.

"What can I do?" I heard the official say. "Just let him go."

We all got back onto the bus and soon crossed the border. Immigration again! The passengers went to have their passports stamped. I waited outside. There were a great many beggars – children of my own age, blind people, old people. "My friend, give me one kwacha! My friend, give me one kwacha!"

I hated it. It felt as though I were the one begging. I couldn't believe that even in a country like Mozambique children were forced to beg from foreigners. Were they not supposed to be at school? Didn't children go to school in free countries?

I felt about for the last coins I had and called the children. "Take this. Take this," I said, handing out the coins.

I kept handing out coins until I had none left. Then I waited at the bus while the other passengers had their passports checked, not knowing what to expect. "Be on your guard," one of the bystanders warned me as I waited. "The police don't mean well."

Eventually, it was time to board the bus again. Two policemen came and stood by the door of the bus to check that everyone had had their passport stamped. I kept changing my position in the line of passengers boarding the bus until everyone else had got on, then I attempted to slip past the policemen.

"Where is your mother?" one of them demanded as I made a dash for the door.

I told him that I had no mother. I was from Sudan.

"Get out!"

The bus was about to pull off, but the passengers were shouting, "Wait! Wait for the boy!"

One of the policemen went back to consult the immigration officer. He came out of his office and called, "Where is John Garang from Sudan?"

My name is Aher, or Santino but John Garang was the name of the Sudanese rebel leader – and a term used to address any Sudanese male whose name you do not know – so I went up to him.

He gave me an encouraging pat on the shoulder. "Promise that you will keep up the struggle," he said. "Get in. Good luck."

Everyone on the bus applauded.

After that every single person on the bus wanted to be my friend and share their food with me.

* * *

We travelled all day until, at five o'clock, we reached the border with Zimbabwe.

"Come, hold my passport for me," said a big mama as we approached immigration.

"Wait for me by the fence," she told me as soon as we were through immigration.

While she went to buy me a Coke, three other mamas brought

some rice and hard-boiled eggs from the bus and sat down with me. "You are welcome to eat with us," they said.

Many other passengers also brought me drinks.

When all the passports had been shown the driver called me to board the bus first. How nice it was to be heading for Harare, knowing that I had safely passed through the final barrier!

It was nine in the evening when we reached that great city, and it was raining. Apart from myself only two other passengers alighted. The rest were going on to Beit Bridge and South Africa.

16

The bus had dropped me at the railway station. Crowds of people were coming and going, but I spoke to no one. Instead, I found an unoccupied bench and went to sleep on it. There I remained until the station was deserted and I was evicted.

By the time I groggily followed the security officer outside it was very late. I was alone and all of a sudden I felt afraid. My English was good enough to get by in a refugee camp, but this was Zimbabwe! How would I ever cope?

Outside the station I bumped into a bunch of street kids who addressed me cheerfully in Shona. I was unable to respond, but there was an old man limping along painfully behind them, and it was he who spoke to me in English. He spoke slowly and deliberately so that I might follow his words. "What are you doing here, boy?" he asked. "Where do you sleep?"

"I have only just arrived, sir. I don't know where to sleep," I replied.

"Where do you come from?" he asked.

"From Sudan."

"Sudan?" he repeated. "Now I *am* pleased to meet you. I once had a very good friend who came from Sudan . . . I sleep on the streets myself, so I can't offer you a bed, but you are my guest. Let me take you to the police station. I know the officers. They are very friendly and they will let you spend the night there."

With few other options, I decided to follow the man.

"And tomorrow," he said, as we set off, "I'll show you where the UNHCR is."

When we arrived at the police station he informed the officer at the front desk that I had arrived from Sudan that evening and had no one to help me.

"Thank you for helping this youngster," the officer said with appreciation.

"I'm old," the old man told the officer. "I've seen better days, but this boy is still young and his country is at war. He qualifies for help from the UNHCR." He was visibly disturbed.

I looked at the old man as he stood there shivering with cold. He was barefoot and his coat and trousers were torn and dirty, but I felt privileged to have met such a person. Through his kindness he had made me forget my own troubles.

"Stay here. You can sleep in the hall," the officer told him. "It's the least I can do after the kindness you have shown this boy." Then, turning to me, he asked, "How long have you been travelling? Where did you get the money?"

I told him that I had commenced my journey in Kenya and how my kind friends from Bangladesh and the Congo had paid for almost everything along the way.

"Have you eaten anything since you arrived?" he asked.

"No, sir."

Another officer – by now a number of them had gathered to hear my story – disappeared into a back room and quickly returned with some bread and two plastic glasses of Fanta Orange for the old man and myself. When we had finished eating and drinking they took me to one of the dormitories they had for the homeless. There were many other people inside and it was pretty hard to find a space on a bench, but eventually I managed to find a place to lie down.

At about midnight another old man came in. He sat down near

me. After a while he asked me something in Shona. I looked at him blankly. Immediately, my dark complexion gave me away.

"Are you from Sudan?" he asked.

"Yes."

"When did you arrive?"

"Yesterday."

He dug in his pockets and found some coins. "Do you know these coins?"

"No, sir."

"Do you have any foreign money on you?"

"No, I don't."

He gave me five Zim dollars. "This will come in handy when you get hungry tomorrow," he said.

I thanked my benefactor, feeling that I had been blessed that day. I had received so much without ever having to ask.

* * *

In the morning I was woken by the other people in the dormitory getting up and leaving. I followed the flow to where I found the old man who had brought me to the police station the night before. He was still fast asleep.

I sat down next to him and his eyes opened. "Thank you very much for your help," I said. "Look what I've got!" I showed him the coins the man had given me during the night. "Take them. I give them to you."

"No, thank you, I won't take your money," he said.

"Please, take it!" I insisted. "I don't want to pay you, just to thank you."

But he refused, saying rather grumpily that I would need the coins for food. "To tell the truth, I don't know where the UNHCR is," he admitted, "or any Sudanese place I can take you to. Perhaps the police will be able to help you."

When he was gone I went to the counter to make sure they hadn't forgotten about me. "Don't worry," an officer reassured me. "Just wait on that bench over there. Someone will come to take you to the UNHCR."

But I soon got bored just sitting there in that gloomy room with no one to talk to. The sun was shining outside and I got up and wandered off, through the gate and into the street, touching the coins in my pocket. To my surprise the buildings were not as high as those in Nairobi, not as close together, and all built in different styles.

When, on my way back from the city centre, I passed the same building for the fourth time I realised that I was lost. A kind lady directed me to the UNICEF offices. There were two guards at the gate. "Good morning, sirs," I said.

"Morning to you," they replied.

I just stood there until one of them asked, "John Garang, how can we help you?"

I explained in my best English that I had arrived the night before and knew no one in Harare. Perhaps someone in the UNICEF offices would be able to help me.

"Two of your brothers have just passed by on their way to the SPLA offices," the guard informed me. "You'd better go there. Come, let me give you the address."

He jotted it down on a slip of paper: 14 Phillips Avenue, Belgravia.

"Follow this road until you get to Phillips Avenue, then turn left. The first gate is theirs. Just knock."

I did as I had been told. Some distance down the street I saw a sign: Embassy of Sudan. Sudan! It felt as though I had come home! But then I saw the flag. It was red and black. It was the northern Sudanese embassy. I'd better not knock on that door!

I ran back to the watchmen.

"Didn't you find the place?" the guard who had given me directions asked.

"The place you told me about isn't the SPLA offices, it's the Arab embassy. They are the enemy. They'll do something horrible to me if they see me. Let me go and speak to your receptionist."

He laughed. "Listen, I'll direct you once more," he said. "Go straight past the Arab embassy to Phillips Avenue. That is the place for blacks like you."

I crept past the Arab embassy, keeping my eyes down.

* * *

A soldier holding a gun stood guard at the gate of 14 Phillips Avenue. "Is this the SPLA offices, sir?" I asked suspiciously.

"Yes," he replied. "Haven't you been here before?"

"No. I only arrived last night."

"Well, you are welcome."

He wrote my name in his file and told me that I would find some of my brothers inside.

As I approached the door I saw the real flag – black, white, red, white and green – waving in the breeze. What a relief! I couldn't help but laugh with joy.

I found my two brothers from Sudan in the waiting room. They rose and embraced me, welcoming me. Grabbing my hands, they led me to a chair and made me sit down. "Hey, jijamer, how far have you been breaking the bush?" the older one asked. The name "jijamer," the Arabic word for "minor" or "Red Army", had been given to us in Panyido and would remain ours forever.

"All the way from Nairobi," I replied.

"Well, we are happy that you arrived here safely," he said, laughing. "Did you come alone or were you travelling with someone?"

"Alone."

The younger one then went off to fetch me some Coke. "Cool your throat first and then you can tell us your story," the older one said.

I took two sips and placed the glass on the table. Then they introduced themselves: the older man was Koul and the younger one Paul Wol, both from Bahr el Ghazal, Dinka-speaking like me.

"I saw you at the minors' camp at Kakuma," Paul said. "How nice to have you here with us! God brought you here in good health."

"I was in Egypt," Koul told me. "When I had raised enough money I caught a plane to Zimbabwe."

We passed the time talking.

"We are staying at the Refugee Transit Centre," Paul told me. "Dr Benjamin is our representative. We're waiting for him to see us. Why don't you take a shower in the bathroom over there and when we've talked to him we'll take you to the UNHCR."

After my shower, I found Koul waiting to introduce me to the representative, who was sitting outside in his car.

"Dr Benjamin, this is Aher, the young man we were telling you about," Koul said as he made his way into the car park. "Can you believe it, such a young boy breaking the bush by himself?"

I guess Dr Benjamin was in no mood to welcome anyone that day. Perhaps he didn't approve of the way Koul introduced me, but he didn't even bother to look at me. Instead, he put a limp hand through the open car window for me to shake. "Take him to the UNHCR offices. That's where refugees go. No one's invited you to come to the movement's offices," he said.

I was taken aback. I was accustomed to my own people treating me with the consideration due to someone who had suffered much in the war. This important man with his doctorate did not impress me at all.

Paul looked crestfallen. "What's wrong, Paul?" I asked when the representative had driven off.

"Nothing seems to have changed since the days we were dodging the Arabs' bombs," he said. "I can't tell you too much now, but please know that you are still in the bush even though you are surrounded by tall buildings and fast cars. Don't think that we, who have fled our homeland, have escaped suffering."

Paul then offered to accompany me to the UNHCR offices while Koul went on ahead to tell the boys at the Refugee Transit Centre that I had arrived in Harare.

* * *

The receptionist at the UNHCR offices was very friendly. "Oh, welcome," she said, when Paul introduced me. "There's a chair for you. Please wait there."

Paul asked to be excused as he also had to get back to the Refugee Transit Centre. "Don't worry about me," I assured him. "I'll speak my best English."

After Paul had left the receptionist brought me some forms to fill in.

"Can you write in English?" she asked.

"Yes, ma'am."

"Well, fill in these forms and bring them back to me when you have finished."

Later, she returned with some bread and tea, which was very welcome.

When I handed her my forms, she looked pleased. "There's a war in Sudan and yet you have learned to write so well!" she said.

I stood talking to her until the driver from the transit centre arrived in a white Toyota to collect me and the supplies I had been given – two kilograms of sugar, ten kilograms of maize meal and some other good things to eat.

The centre was only a five-minute drive away, but I enjoyed every minute – I had never been in a car like that before.

When we arrived at the centre Koul and the boys were waiting at the main gate to welcome me – among them were Angok and Bol Bol who, along with me, had been in the group of seven at Ifo who had missed being resettled in America. The driver had instructions to take me straight to administration, so he didn't stop, but I waved to them and they came running after the car.

17

"Hello, John Garang," the administrator of the Refugee Transit Centre said.

I smiled and returned his greeting.

He paged through the new file on his desk and asked me some questions before telling me that I was going to stay with my peers from Sudan. "There are lots of Sudanese boys in the centre," he told me.

I was given four blankets and two buckets. The manager then escorted me to the door, carrying the blankets himself, and called a boy to assist me. I could hardly believe my eyes. Chol! My best friend, Chol Biem, from Ifo!

Chol rushed to embrace me.

"Chol! Jijamer! How have you been?" I asked.

"Hey, jijamer, nothing good! Just struggling." The same old Chol; still short, still confident.

"Welcome! Welcome!" Many other boys came to greet me. Though I didn't know all their names, I recognised faces from various groups.

They helped me carry my belongings to the Sudanese quarters. It was great to be among friends who were happy to see me.

Everyone wanted to know how I had managed to get to Harare. They told me their stories too. Their journeys, it seemed, had been far more arduous than mine. A few had even spent a month in a Tanzanian prison.

We talked the night away, debating many topics. We laughed a lot, and cried.

Then the conversation turned to a certain person who claimed to represent the SPLA in Zimbabwe, but was pursuing his own interests. He objected to our coming to the place where he himself had taken refuge, my friends told me.

"It's because of him that many of our applications for asylum are being turned down by the government here. He's hand in glove with them. We know some boys who have been denied refugee status because they are relatives of a politician he happens to bear a grudge against."

"He keeps asking us why we are running away from the fighting in Sudan. 'Who will fight the war?' he asks us. Meanwhile, he has been living in Harare for eleven years, miles from danger, safe in his big residence!"

"His children can't even speak their own mother tongue!"

"One of his sons is in the US doing his masters. Another one is at a university in Namibia. And the third one is in Form IV in Zimbabwe."

"His daughter is a model in America!"

"They know nothing about Sudan or Sudanese traditions!"

"Have they suffered in any war?"

These boys despised Dr Benjamin. "He keeps accusing us of cowardice because we have fled the war in Sudan, because we refuse to enlist in the army now that we have grown up."

I was shocked. I had seen my friends fighting starvation in numerous refugee camps and I knew that they were certainly not cowards.

"Haven't you received any assistance at all from the SPLA offices?" I asked.

"You will see for yourself what kind of representative he is," someone answered bitterly. "We can forget about ever achieving any of our goals if Zimbabwe deports us. And they will, because the one who has been appointed to protect us has become our enemy."

It was past two in the morning when we turned in.

* * *

At eight the next morning I was summoned to the immigration office to apply for a temporary permit.

A refugee's position in Zimbabwe was precarious. You had to apply for refugee status, and, in consultation with the UNHCR, the government would determine your fate. It was no secret why so many Sudanese boys were denied refugee status – Dr Benjamin was, as I had been told, hand in glove with the Zimbabwean government. And if you appealed to the government after you had been turned down, your case would merely be referred back to Dr Benjamin, a man who seemed intent on providing the rebel army with a steady supply of new recruits. "Why are you running away from the war?" he kept saying. "If you need help, I can give you enough money to get back to the warzone. But if you are looking for an education without having been nominated, well, I'm sorry!"

He must have regarded himself as a Hero of the Movement.

My friend Chol and I were lucky. At fourteen we were still minors and our applications were processed without the assistance of the Hero. Within two months we received our refugee status – which entitled us to a monthly allowance of five hundred Zim dollars for accommodation and food. It did, however, also mean that we would have to leave the Refugee Transit Centre and look for a place to rent.

With two other boys – Angok and Awang – we found a room in

Eastlea big enough to share with the others who hadn't received an allowance. Of course, there were also those boys whose applications had been rejected and who were looking for financial assistance to get to South Africa. We did what we could to help them too.

We were expected to attend school, and there were sponsors, but the officials in charge kept telling us, "We can't find you schools. Just bring us proof of admission and we'll pay your school fees and give you a monthly allowance. You have six months to come up with a school, then our offer will lapse."

So it was up to each boy to find a school that was prepared to admit him. This was a tall order as Zimbabwean schools required a birth certificate and, in addition, the child's parents to be present when he or she was enrolled. We had neither birth certificates nor parents.

We kept running from school to school till at last, in June 1998, I, Chol Biem, Awang and two others were admitted to the David Livingstone Primary School, which offered night classes for high school students. After four months I passed my Form III. We were indeed privileged.

The situation many other Sudanese refugees found themselves in was deteriorating fast. Whereas many migrants from other countries – the DRC, Burundi, Rwanda and Somalia – were granted refugee status, few Sudanese were so fortunate. In addition, the organisations providing aid to our community were finding it increasingly difficult to cope with the influx of Sudanese refugees, so that newcomers were no longer being given the assistance we had received. Although our allowances were cut, too, we were not permitted to return to the transit centre.

The boys who did have a little money would rent the best rooms they could afford and allow six or seven others to crowd in. This, however, was against the law and pitiless landlords kept us moving from place to place.

Obtaining food posed another problem, particularly after the last of our companions had moved out of the transit centre and no longer received any supplies to share with us.

Chol and I didn't blame the Zimbabwean government for our dilemma. They had, after all, granted us refugee status and some financial assistance. But the SPLA representative! The man who was supposed to understand the roots of our misery was betraying us. His movement was no longer our movement; he treated us like the enemy.

Whenever we went to a church or NGO to beg for assistance they would say something like, "But only yesterday we made a donation to your representative, who had appealed to us on your behalf. How come you are still hungry?"

Our fury grew. Who was Dr Benjamin, after all? How could he expect to enjoy power without the support of the people? And how could he count on us to support him?

Finally, one afternoon, we invaded the building – I was still sharing accommodation in Eastlea with Angok and Awang, but many of the other boys had run out of money and had nowhere to stay. Immediately, Dr Benjamin shouted for the Zimbabwean guards. "Remove these boys!" he ordered.

But they were on our side and whenever Dr Benjamin gave them orders to remove us they just ignored him. Some even had the courage to respond to him by saying, "Ambassador, how do we know the enemies of this office? You confuse us by allowing Arabs in here and pushing out these boys who you should be protecting. Our job is to protect you from the Arabs. These boys are not Arab."

18

Then came the great demonstration, staged outside the UNHCR offices by refugees from many countries. It lasted for two days. I was aware of them, but I wasn't involved. I wasn't even sure what they were protesting against as I was attending school.

Early on the second day of the demonstration, a Saturday, my friend Awang and I were on our way to play football, carrying our boots and socks in a small school bag. Little did we know that it was to be our unlucky day.

The previous night some refugees, who had occupied the UNHCR building, had been attacked by the police. There were many casualties. Some had been bitten by dogs, others beaten.

Blissfully unaware of these developments, Awang and I were walking along when we were pounced upon by three police officers, who ordered us to get into their van.

"What is the problem, sirs?" we asked. "Sirs, why are you arresting us?"

"Do you want to tell me that you don't know what is going on between the police and you refugees?" one of the officers barked. "Get into the van. You will find out soon enough."

We noticed that several police vehicles had appeared while we had been talking and had begun moving up and down the street, rounding up refugees. Intimidated by all the activity we obediently got into the back of the van. Unfortunately, we were not alone. There were several ferocious-looking dogs in the van – behind bars, but still! "There are dogs in there!" we protested, scrambling out again.

"You people! You think you can dictate to us. Get in!" another officer ordered.

We climbed in. The dogs were so wild that I thought they would break out of their cage, but I felt slightly more secure when two of the police officers got into the back of the van with us.

Ten minutes later we were travelling through an industrial area, on our way to the Refugee Transit Centre, when the driver stopped to assist a police officer who was wrestling with someone on the roadside. Our van stopped – in the middle lane – and the three officers in the front of the van jumped out. The two who had been sitting with us followed, leaving Awang and me alone. The minute they had gone the dogs broke out of their cage and came for us. I jumped out and ran in the direction of the officers, hoping they would come to my rescue, but the stationary van had caused a traffic jam, blocking me from reaching the policemen. I was pushed over by one of the dogs. Awang was knocked over too and fell across my legs. Cars were hooting. Suddenly there were three dogs on me and four on Awang. I rolled over onto my back, trying to protect my throat, my leg being mangled by one of the dogs.

The first officer to reach us was not one of the handlers, so he was attacked too. Then the handlers arrived, and just in time. They called the dogs off, but the one whose fangs were stuck in my leg wouldn't let go. I had to grab hold of his jaws myself, with my fingers against his teeth, and force his mouth open.

Awang got up slowly, ignoring his own pain to come to my aid. I rose too, pulling up my trouser leg to inspect my wound. There was no blood. My leg was swollen and very white. Then the blood gushed out.

The police called for an ambulance, but were told to take me to the transit centre, where all the ambulances were already waiting. This was it, I thought. This was the injury that was going to kill me.

But when we reached the ambulances and I became aware of those whose injuries were far worse than mine I resigned myself to waiting my turn. Eventually, I joined five other people in an ambulance. Two were lying on stretchers and three were sitting on a bench. Serious cases were being loaded into three other ambulances. There was a man from the DRC who had had the muscle torn off his leg by a dog, and a Rwandan man with a gaping wound in his head, a wound inflicted by a baton.

We joined the men, women and children waiting for medical attention at the hospital. The most critical cases obviously had to be attended to first. I was handed some cotton wool with which to stop the bleeding and a bandage to wind around my leg. Eventually, a doctor came to give me an injection. I was to return for follow-up injections until the beginning of 1999. Luckily, Awang was not so badly hurt.

19

The life of a refugee is truly hard. You are manipulated by greedy politicians. You are abused, disempowered and mocked by citizens who do not recognise your humanity.

An elder in Panyido camp once spoke to me and some other minors about this. He was one of several severely disabled patients who lay day after day on their backs in the clinic with plastic tubes protruding from all parts of their bodies. What was it, I wondered, that enabled him, in this pitiful condition, to associate on equal terms with able-bodied men?

One day a friend of mine and I asked him.

"God is the creator of us all," he explained. "When you see a disabled person, don't cry for him or laugh at him, he is the product of God's love and the destruction of war.

"I do admit that it is easy to hate others if you are ashamed of your own mutilated body," he continued, "especially if people cease to respect your dignity and your worth. So you boys should be sensitive when you encounter a disabled person like me. Respect us and we will be consoled by the knowledge that even if we die from the injuries inflicted by the Arabs there will be children like you to perpetuate our dreams. We shall also know that our pain has not been in vain, but has been necessary to secure a better world for you, our children.

"You, who have two legs, should never laugh at a man limping along on one. Honour him!"

Then he told us a story.

"There was once a great forest," he said, "in an area that was notorious for its warring tribes. Warriors who were killed in battle were not buried, but left for the birds and beasts to feed on. Bare skulls lay scattered among the trees.

"One day a brave man was making his way through the forest on his way to visit some friends on the other side. Noticing two skulls lying in the footpath, he stopped to address one of them. 'You, pitiful skull, I know what it was that killed you!' he said. 'It was your own brain, the problems in your mind. Why are you just lying there, skinless? Why aren't you doing something about those problems?'

"And with that he kicked the skull out of his way.

"But as he was about to leave, the skull turned and answered. 'Go,' it told the brave man, 'but you too will be hounded by the problems in *your* head.'

"The brave man was shocked. Was the skull speaking to him? Was it telling him that he too had a mental illness? And that he would not be able to escape it?

"'Go away!' he shouted at the skull. 'Do you think that I'm like you, that I will die here in the middle of the forest without parents to bury me? Don't waste my time.'

"'Go on your way,' the skull said, 'but you'll see, you too will be afflicted by a problem created in your own head.'

"All the way to the village the brave man's thoughts were indeed disturbed. A skull had spoken to him in the dark forest! And despite the fact that he was a brave man the thought made him hurry on towards the village.

"When he reached the village the young men, all warriors, were playing a noisy game under the trees.

"'Please!' he shouted. 'Be quiet! There is something I must tell you.'

"Expecting to hear good news, the men gathered round him. 'Tell us,' they said.

"The brave man had lowered his head, waiting for them to calm down. When they were finally silent he looked up. 'I was coming through the forest when I found two skulls lying in the road,' he said. 'You know how many heads there are in the forest. All of a sudden one of them started talking to me.'

"'Liar! Go away! A skull can't talk!' the men replied.

"'I'm serious,' the brave man continued. 'It did talk. If this is a lie, you can kill me too. Come on, I'll show you.'

"'All right,' the young men said, 'we'll go back with you. But it's a long way, and if this skull of yours doesn't answer you we'll kill you on the spot, as you said.'

"When they reached the two skulls the men gathered expectantly around them. The brave man kicked the skull. 'You, skull, you who were killed by your own mind, tell these people what you told me,' he said.

"There was no sound.

"'Make it talk,' the men demanded. 'You said you could.'

"The brave man turned to the skull again, insisting that it speak to him, but the skull did not respond. He tried the second skull, but there was no answer.

"'You liar!' the men said. 'What did we tell you? Skulls don't talk. You have wasted our time.'

"'I'm telling you, the skull talked to me,' the brave man replied.

"'We are going to kill you.'

"'Please,' the brave man pleaded, 'it wasn't a lie.'

"But the men were in no mood to argue and slaughtered the brave man where he stood.

"Just as the men were leaving the skull started laughing. 'I told you!' it said. 'It was *your* mind that was disturbed, not mine. You thought you could mock a skull lying unburied in the forest, did you?' The men from the village stood transfixed. 'And you, you couldn't believe your own ears, could you?' the skull said, addressing them. 'A skull talking, indeed!'

"They fled for their lives, but the brave man's body remained in the forest, another head to keep the first two company."

My friend and I gaped at the old man.

"Why have I told you such a horrible story?" he asked. "This world is such a wilderness that you can't go around mocking the misfortunes and disabilities of others, whether they have been caused by war or nature. Remember to always show respect to others, whoever they are. Your mothers and fathers are not here to talk to you, so I will tell you: in our culture no one is permitted to abuse young children. And, in return, you children should never abuse anyone."

20

I was *not* going to stay in bed. That would be too much like suffering and I had had enough of suffering. Anyway, there wouldn't be anyone to take care of me if I did. With my trousers covering my sore leg I hobbled out into the world to look for food – and for education, which I craved.

Up until 1998 my schooling was sponsored by the UNHCR through the International Catholic Migration Commission, but the ICMC had now informed us that after 1998 they would no longer be able to pay our school fees if we attended private schools. Neither could they negotiate with government schools on our behalf. If we could get a government school to admit us, and brought the admission form as proof, then fine, they would continue to support us. Otherwise, our allowances for school fees, food and accommodation would be cancelled.

Didn't they know that no government school would admit a child without a birth certificate? It was the law.

Boys from Sudan, the Congo, Rwanda and Burundi kept meeting one another in the lobbies of government schools every day, each hoping that he would be the lucky one to be admitted, but we were always floored by the same demand: "Show me your birth certificate."

There was a mission school – Visitation High School – that many of the boys had already tried unsuccessfully, but as I was running out of options I thought that I would go and speak to them anyway.

The first thing I noticed on arrival was a sign outside the door of the receptionist's office: *Sorry, we have no vacancies for Forms III to VI.*

I entered anyway. "Good morning, madam," I said.

"Good morning to you. How can I help you?" the woman behind the desk asked.

"Please, I want a space for next year."

"I am sorry to tell you that we have no more spaces for next year," she said. "There's a notice outside."

"I *want* a space! Not very polite!" said a voice behind me.

It was the headmaster, standing in the door to his office. He was an elderly man with neatly trimmed grey hair and a moustache. "You can't just say, 'I *want* a space'," he continued. "That would be forcing this lady to admit you. Is that what you want to do?"

I smiled meekly. "Oh, no, sir. I'm not trying to force her. I'm just asking politely if there is a space."

"Well ask again, properly," he said.

I tried my best: "Madam, may I ask you to find me a space in Form IV, please?"

"'May' is better than 'want'," the headmaster commented, "but 'need' would be an even better word to use: 'I need a space.' But tell me, where are you from? Why isn't there an adult with you?"

"I'm Sudanese," I told him. "I was separated from my parents in the war. I don't know what's become of them."

"Then who will pay your school fees?" he asked.

"The UNHCR, sir."

"But why aren't they looking for a school on your behalf?" he asked. "How will you ever find a school by yourself?"

"It's difficult, sir, but I've had to take care of myself since 1987."

"If you'll excuse me, I'll take this boy to my office," the headmaster told the receptionist.

113

In his office the headmaster offered me a seat and poured me a cup of tea. Then he went off to attend to some business. My heart was pounding.

"I am a refugee, myself," he told me when he returned. "At least, I was one in Tanzania during the Zimbabwean war. I know how difficult a refugee's life can be. Listen, it is true that we are not taking any more new students, but since you are a refugee I'll see what I can do. Mind you, I can't promise anything. The priests are in charge of administration. They will decide. Do you have a birth certificate?"

"No, sir," I replied.

"Any proof that you have passed Form III?"

"I've got a report from my school in Kenya, sir."

"Well, don't count on me. Keep trying to find a space elsewhere. But give me your phone number and address, and, if there's good news, I'll call you."

It was with a light heart that I walked past the receptionist. She made a remark about the boy who had tried to force her to admit him and we both laughed.

It was too late to visit any more schools that afternoon, so I joined my friends. None of them had had any success.

The next day we went back to the UNHCR where we once again explained why the schools refused to admit us and begged them to help us. "Wait till next year," was all they said. "We'll pay the school fees of any boy who is admitted."

Nothing had changed and there was no peace between us and the UNHCR. We were well aware that the UN had made money available for our education. Why were they stalling? The year was approaching its end and we were in danger of losing our already reduced grants.

21

That night I couldn't sleep. I lay on my bed, recalling every move
I had made since those early days in Panyido – Gilo River, Pochella,
the Mountain of Punishment, Corchuey, Lokichokio, Kakuma,
Ifo, the trip to Zimbabwe. I prayed. That night I prayed many times,
asking God for many things. I begged Him to guard my parents,
wherever they were, and I prayed for my country. For Sudan.
And for the whole suffering world. I lay awake for many hours,
worrying about my schooling. Would I ever wear a school uniform
again? I wondered. I simply had to enrol in a school before the
end of the year.

During the early hours of the morning it occurred to me that
God had never forsaken me. He had brought me safely through
the crossfire at Gilo River. He had sent friends to help me find my
way to Zimbabwe. Hopefully, I thought, the same God who had
brought me so far would help me to get a proper education. It is
possible that He had created me for a purpose, that I had a mission
on this earth.

I would leave it in the hands of the Lord, I decided.

But all of a sudden I was angry again. Furious! A mission? It was
the futility of life as a refugee that was so utterly frustrating! How
I hated it! Bitten by a dog! Had I not been a refugee, I would have
sued the police. But as a refugee I knew my efforts would only
end in fruitless arguments about whether I had taken part in the
demonstration outside the UNHCR. I knew I would just have to
accept that this was what had happened and get on with my life.
In the morning, when I approached yet another school, I would

have to be a good person – courteous, like the men I respected –
and not like those stupid policemen whose dogs had mangled
my leg!

22

At dawn I took a shower, washed my tears away, dressed and braced myself for another day.

That morning I did at last succeed in getting a government school to accept my application, but their fees were high, much higher than the mission school's. Not much hope that my sponsor would approve of that, I thought. But as they had insisted on my finding a government school I resolved to show them the form the receptionist had handed me. If they didn't like it, let them sponsor me at a private school!

My companions, meanwhile, had succeeded in finding us some food and they also had some good news for me. "The headmaster of Visitation High School called," they told me as soon as I opened the door. "He wants you to collect your admission forms for Form IV today."

Wow!

Back at Visitation High School the headmaster welcomed me into his office and handed me a list of everything I would need. The school fees were 5 720 Zim dollars and with uniforms, bedclothes and everything else the total came to around 18 000 Zim dollars.

"Thank you, sir. I'm not sure that my sponsor will accept this," I told him, "but I'll come back to tell you. Meanwhile, please reserve the space for me. I appreciate everything you have done for me."

God had heard my prayer! It was true that He was there for me. Outside the school I stopped in the shade of a big tree and thanked Him.

When I got back home my friends congratulated me and wished me good luck for the interview with our reluctant sponsor. I went to bed early so that I might be fresh the next day.

The following morning, at the UNHCR offices, I showed the UN Refugee Education Director – the woman whose job it was to see to our education – the form from the government school. She was perplexed. "But this government school is even more expensive than the private schools!" she exclaimed. "You'd better go and look for a cheaper government school."

"I've got another admission form, ma'am," I said. "It's from a mission school. Visitation High School. Here it is."

She examined it. "Yes, it *is* cheaper, but it's not a government school. All right, I'll submit both forms to the committee. The mission school might not be such a bad idea after all. Come back in a week's time."

If this application failed, I thought as I left her office, it would mean that the UNHCR was just not interested in helping us at all and I would have to look elsewhere for a sponsor.

* * *

"I am sorry," the woman told me a week later. "Both have been rejected. Unless you can find a cheaper school we can't help you."

I was up in arms. "Is your office committed to helping refugees or not?" I demanded.

"We *are* helping you," she replied. "I would be only too happy to assist you if you could find a cheaper school."

"Could you give me the name of a cheaper school?" I asked.

"Actually, no," she replied, returning my two forms to me.

I bade her farewell and went to see the Commissioner for Refugees. I explained my problem to him and showed him my two admission forms. "But the committee has discussed your case," he exclaimed, "and they have decided to sponsor you at the mission school. Perhaps the director has forgotten. We thought it would be the better option as it's a boarding school. We were hoping that they would let us sponsor more children there. But wait, I'll remind her."

With that he picked up the telephone, called the director and cleared up the misunderstanding.

"Go back to her office," he instructed me after he had finished on the telephone. "You are going to the mission school."

I found the director scrutinising her copies of my admission papers. "All right," she said. "You can go to your mission school. But let me make one thing clear: we cannot afford to buy all the items on this list. We'll pay for two pairs of trousers, not three. Two shirts, one pair of shoes, one blazer and one winter T-shirt. No blankets or sportswear or pyjamas. If you want more, you'll have to buy it yourself. You refugees give yourself airs! I can't even afford to send my own children to a fancy mission school."

She was jealous of me! But I didn't want to argue with her, so I just nodded.

Then she informed me that my monthly allowance for food and accommodation would be discontinued. I was to receive nothing for the remaining two months of the year. I could eat again when I got to school, she told me.

That was the limit! "Could you please put all these conditions in writing?" I asked her, hoping that the Commissioner for Refugees might once again intervene, but she refused.

* * *

Could the UN Refugee Education Director be serious about cutting off my allowance? I wasn't convinced that she could be that cruel, but when, on 25 November, I found myself at the head of the queue of minors waiting for their money I realised that she really had been serious: I got nothing at all, nothing I could use for rent or food.

Reluctantly, I joined the ranks of those who were struggling by without the assistance of the woman who called herself the UN Refugee Education Director.

Without my allowance I knew I would have to move out of the room I had been sharing with two friends, but when I told them of my predicament it quickly became clear that without my contribution they would have to move too. We hoped to find shelter in the offices of the movement, but our countryman Dr Benjamin was up to his usual tricks. As soon as we showed our faces he called the police to remove us and five other boys who were also looking for a place to stay. After my experience with the dogs earlier in the year, the police didn't need to use force. The three of us left and headed for the suburb of Waterfalls, where some boys we knew rented a cottage, while the other five remained to pursue their little rebellion.

It was late when we got to our friends' cottage. They invited us in, and although the room was small, seven of us managed to find space to sleep on the floor.

In the morning the boys we had left behind at the movement's offices joined us. We pooled our cash and found that we would be able to rent a second small cottage in the same area, although this would leave us no cash at all for food.

Some days later we bumped into two guys who had just arrived in Harare and had been put up at the Refugee Transit Centre.

They shared their rations with us and, assisted by the friendly security guards, smuggled me into the centre to share their room.

Once again I found myself casting about for money. I didn't want to present myself at Visitation High School in January without everything I needed. I was lucky. Stanley, a friend of mine who was working for the Jesuit Refugee Services in Harare, promised to let me have 3 000 Zim dollars when he received his salary.

When the festive season arrived very few boys we knew had school to look forward to in the coming year, but we wished one another a merry Christmas anyway. "If only our brothers from the minors' group in Sudan could see us now!" one of my companions remarked, laughing grimly. "They think we are enjoying the good life here. We should get the media to show them how hungry we are!"

"Oh, well, it's better than having bombs dropped on you on Christmas Day," someone replied.

Our landlord lent us some money and we bought food as well as a pack of playing cards to keep us occupied until the new year arrived.

* * *

I was to present myself at Visitation High School on 5 January 1999 and did not want anything to go wrong. I went to the UNHCR offices to check everything had been done properly. They showed me a receipt, proving that my school fees had been paid. As for my uniform, I would have to wait until the seventh, when the director would be able to take me and some other boys to the wholesalers to purchase what we needed. I rushed to my friend at the Jesuit Refugee Services offices, but he told me that he wouldn't have any money in his bank account until the fifteenth.

What could I do? I couldn't face the other students without a uniform.

The fifth came and went. On the sixth I phoned the headmaster.

"Don't worry," he said. "Do what you can. The school will donate what you cannot afford to buy. And I will reserve your place for six months."

I realised that I would have to be cautious. I was a foreigner and I was unsure of the reception the students would give me. I would have to rely on the headmaster for support, behave courteously towards the other students and work hard. Meanwhile, I could only wait patiently for my sponsor to buy me a uniform, while trying to survive in the company of my penniless peers.

When the seventh arrived, I accepted whatever the director bought me without argument. On the fifteenth my Sudanese brother, Stanley, gave me the 3 000 Zim dollars he had promised me – enough to purchase the rest of the items I needed: two blankets, two sheets, pyjamas, a pillow and a trunk. I even got a little change.

23

I had everything I needed, but I was still feeling strangely uneasy. I was a new boy and I was arriving late. It would be hugely embarrassing to go walking up the path towards the school, lugging a large trunk, with all the children watching me. My Sudanese brothers had been impressed by my trunk and everything in it – "You may be hungry, but it doesn't show," they assured me. "A proper schoolboy!" – but they also understood my uneasiness. They advised me to leave the trunk with them, as it was too large for my clothes and I wasn't taking any food. "Put your clothes in two plastic bags," they said. "You can always collect your trunk later."

Saturday and Sunday passed slowly. On Monday, 18 January a bus dropped me near my destination. Dressed in school uniform, and carrying my two bags, I walked towards the school. I was lucky. The students were at lunch and there was nobody in sight. Not even a teacher. I hurried to the headmaster's office. He welcomed me cordially and invited me to join the rest of the school in the dining hall.

I must have looked as embarrassed as I felt, for he changed his mind. "Okay, wait here," he said. "I'll get you something to eat here in my office."

While I waited for the headmaster to return with the food I watched the noisy boys and girls emerging from the dining hall, laughing and fooling about. I wanted them to notice me, but was too shy to show myself. In the end, I just stood there in the headmaster's office, staring at the boys with whom, for a year, I would be sharing life at the school.

After I had finished my food the headmaster went to call the boarding master to take me to the boys' hostel.

In the meantime, some boys and girls came wandering into the reception area. "There's a new boy in the headmaster's office," the receptionist told them. "He's a foreigner."

One or two walked past the door and peeped in, pretending to want to see the headmaster. "Hi!" said one. Some of the others waved at me.

"Hello," I responded tentatively. They looked quite friendly!

Then I heard a student telling his friends outside, "Hey, we've got a new boy, a foreigner. He's in the headmaster's office. Form III or IV, I guess."

A number of boys came to the door to speak to me. "Are you in Form III?" one asked. "Then you'll be in our class."

"You'd be welcome in our class," another said. "Form IV."

The headmaster returned with the boarding master. "Go back to your classes," he immediately told the children, but when he saw how pleased everyone looked, he turned to me. "Would you like to greet your fellow students first?" he asked. "You may leave your bags here."

It was great to meet them. The boys came to shake my hand, while the girls hovered in the background, watching me casually. Everyone was talking at the same time: "What's your name?", "In which form are you? Three or four?", "Where are you from?", "I'm John . . .", "I'm Daniel . . ."

I could only laugh.

When the noise had subsided somewhat, I introduced myself: "I'm Santino, from Sudan."

"What does he say?" someone at the back asked.

"He says he's Santino, from Sudan," someone else replied.

"Okay, children," the boarding master said, picking up my bags. "Back to your classes."

Two boys, who had been chosen to accompany us, took my bags from him as we made our way to the hostel – a single-storey building with clean white walls and a grey corrugated-iron roof. The headmaster had arranged for me to share a room with two prefects and my companions showed me where the showers and toilets were and gave me a copy of the timetable and school rules. "The boys will show you the rest later," the boarding master said. "Now, you'd better join your class."

I was taken to Form IV, where I would stay until the authorities had made up their minds as to where I actually belonged. "You are welcome, Santino," the teacher said and indicated where I should sit.

The lesson lasted until four o'clock, when it was time for sport. Some of my new friends took me to see the sports fields. The students looked so smart in their sportswear – white T-shirts and grey shorts. They were playing basketball and football. Some were even practising athletics. I was introduced to a priest who gave me some Coke and chips. The boys with me were excited and talkative – all but one, a quiet youngster who looked as though he could do with some attention. I gave him my Coke and chips.

It was all rather confusing. Everyone appeared to like me, but one of my new friends had a warning for me. "Be careful!" he said. "There are boys among us who cannot be trusted, even though they may seem to be nice enough now."

"Who?" I asked.

"Just be careful," he repeated.

"My roommates, are they to be trusted?" I asked my new friend on our way back to the hostel to shower and prepare for supper.

They had been pointed out to me on the sports fields, playing volleyball, but I hadn't had the opportunity to meet them.

"Yes," said my companion. "They are good people. They are responsible."

The boarding master was waiting to introduce me to them. "Patson Garisa, prefect, and Semba Rachel, prefect," he said. "They are fine boys. If you have any problems, and I'm not around, they will assist you."

When he had gone a number of boys came knocking at our door. Some were sent away by the prefects; others were allowed to come in and talk to me. Some even helped me make my bed.

"Supper is at seven in the dining hall," Patson informed me a little later. "You have to dress nicely for it."

When the siren sounded we all moved to the dining hall. I was dressed in my new uniform – grey trousers, a green short-sleeved shirt, a white-and-green striped tie and black shoes. Some boys were running to get their supper, but my prefect friends told me not to hurry. It was the custom for the prefects to arrive last and enter when everyone else was seated. The boarding master would find a place for me at a table, they said, but when we entered students were calling from all directions: "Here, Santino!", "Santino, join us!"

I joined a group that looked nice.

The food was brought in on a trolley, grace was said, and soon the noise of spoons on plates was louder even than the din of conversation. There was sadza with meat and vegetables – so much food, in fact, that we were unable to finish it all.

Straight from supper we had to go to our classrooms to study. We were expected to be very quiet and do nothing but work – the teachers were watching from outside. At first I was at a loss what to do as I hadn't yet received any textbooks, but soon someone slipped me a note: *Have you chosen your subjects yet?* it read. *You have to take seven.* Then, more notes arrived, advising me on my options. Some of my classmates wrote questions to test my knowledge. I had to slip my answers back to the senders.

When the last siren of the day sounded the girls returned to their hostel and some boys accompanied me to my room to talk geography. Sleep was no priority, I soon discovered – bedtime was only at midnight – but we were expected to be up at five the next morning to take a shower and brush our teeth so that we were ready for a breakfast of porridge and milk at six.

The next morning I encountered a problem: I did want to look smart, but I didn't have a toothbrush, or Colgate, or soap. A boy caught me under a tree cleaning my teeth with some twigs – a tree brush – and offered me some toothpaste. "Here, use my soap," said someone else in the shower. "I've got plenty."

Everyone was kind. Students and staff treated me very well, but still time passed very slowly for me. I was not particularly sad and not overly happy. I could never forget where I had come from and why I was there, so I just concentrated on working hard. Apart from chess – which we had played in Kakuma and Ifo – I had never learned to play games as a child and this made things difficult, as playing aimless games to while away the time was strange for me. Meanwhile, in the dining hall I didn't want to appear too hungry, so I refrained from eating too much. I also didn't have any tuck like the other boys and was too proud to accept the biscuits and orange drinks they offered me. Then one day Lemson, a boy in Form VI, approached me. "You know, Santino," he said, "the problem with you is that you are much too shy. If you continue to reject gifts, people will think that you don't like them.

I've got to know you quite well and I know you are a friendly guy who likes to interact with people. If it is money you need, I'll lend you some. Return it after the holidays if you are able to. If you aren't, don't worry, I won't mind. You'll find it easier to accept stuff if you have something to offer in return. As for me, I want nothing from you but your friendship."

Lemson wasn't a close friend, but I really appreciated his offer. He was prepared to lend me 500 Zim dollars, but I beat him down to 150, promising to return it after the holidays.

How nice it was to be able to learn from the other children! They took the time to help me overcome my diffidence: when I was too shy to participate freely in the games the children played they made it clear to me that I needed to be more confident. During prep in the evenings I used to receive notes from boys and girls, from Forms I to VI, complimenting me or giving me advice that has stood me in good stead to this day.

In the meantime, Lemson's money enabled me to buy some cool-drinks, biscuits and bread from the tuck shop, so that I could give as well as receive. This made me feel a little bolder.

And the boys I had been warned against – the ones who could not be trusted? I never had any reason to mistrust anyone.

24

When the April holidays arrived eight school buses took those of us who hadn't been collected by our parents into Harare. Dressed in our smart school uniforms we sang songs all the way, and it felt great when the other kids put my name in some of the songs. Another bus from the school overtook ours and I could hear the song they were singing – with my name in it too! I got up and danced with my friends. I was happy. More than happy.

Parents were waiting to meet their children at the Queen Victoria Museum, where we were to be dropped, and as soon as I had said goodbye to my friends I went to my sponsor's office to ask if they would give me an allowance for the holidays. They promised that they would and instructed me to return later.

Thankfully, I then ran into some of my Sudanese brothers, who took me home with them. It was a happy reunion and when I told them about my financial dilemma they immediately clubbed together and handed me 700 Zim dollars. With the promised allowance of 850 more I would be able to buy everything I needed for the following term and repay my debt to Lemson.

I spent that holiday with my Sudanese brothers and when it was time to return to school they escorted me some of the way to the Queen Victoria Museum, carrying my trunk for me. On our way to the museum a number of uniformed boys waved at me from the taxis they were travelling in. "We'd better hire you a taxi too," one of my companions said. And so they did. But when I asked them to come with me they refused as they were embarrassed at the prospect of mingling with boys in uniform.

As I got out of my taxi, I was greeted enthusiastically. "Santino, I would like you to meet my parents," someone called. "Mom, Dad, this is Santino."

"We are so pleased to meet you, Santino," a well-dressed man said, shaking my hand. "My son has told me how proud they all are to have you in their school."

These children seemed happy to know me. If only my parents could have been there too!

May God save my mother and father, wherever they may be, I prayed, my heart beating fast. It's not their fault that I have to cope with life alone.

At least this time I had some cash and I was determined that my best friend would have his money back the minute I saw him.

"Here's your money, Lemson," I said as he appeared out of the crowd. "Thank you. It made all the difference."

"Great of you to return it," he said. "But really, I don't need it just now. It was a gift to you."

"Please take it," I protested.

"No, thanks, but I tell you what, Santino, keep it for the both of us. We may need it later, for sports or something."

From that moment we were truly friends. We shared everything – the contents of our trunks, our money, everything.

Lessons resumed and I joined the public speakers' club. I was even asked to give a speech at assembly one morning. Always I was careful not to spoil my good reputation.

When the next long weekend arrived I made my way back to the house I had shared with my Sudanese brothers during the April holidays. They were gone! Some had left for South Africa, I was told by the landlord, and some for Mozambique.

It was late and I had nowhere to sleep so I headed for Dr Benjamin's office. It was a mistake. Three days earlier a small group of boys had rebelled against his cruel measures. They had gone to his office and demanded to see him. He had refused to speak to them, calling them "the Red Army". I was certainly not welcome there so I wandered up and down the streets of Harare until, at last, I found a nightclub that was open. I spent the rest of the night half-asleep in a chair still dressed in my school uniform.

In the morning I bumped into a school friend, who took me home with him for what remained of the weekend.

Who did Marail Benjamin think we were? It was his fault that I had had to sleep in a nightclub in my school uniform. Let me just finish my school year, I swore, and I would come back to haunt Dr Benjamin.

* * *

Back at school it was soon visitation day. The students' work was displayed in the school hall and the proud parents walked up and down, discussing it with the teachers.

I could see how much their parents' involvement meant to my classmates, but they were also aware of my situation and were very kind to me. As soon as they were allowed to join their parents, they took me along, and all the mothers and fathers made a point of congratulating me on my achievements. After a while I managed to escape to the hostel and locked myself in my room, but it wasn't long before a friend came knocking at my door. He told me that his sister wanted to meet me. Dutifully, I washed my tear-stained face and marched down to where everyone was getting ready for a braai. I hated it! I just wanted to run back to my room, but I had promised my friends that I would be there so their families could meet me and I didn't want to let anyone down.

* * *

The examinations started on 18 October and I wrote my last paper on 2 December. I was really going to miss my friends! They scribbled words of encouragement on my shirt and I wrote on theirs: *Sad for us to part again before we have got to know each other well. One year in this school was like one week to us.*

My last meal at that school consisted of rice and chicken. "Look," I told my friends, "a chicken leg! A leg to help me walk back to Sudan from Zimbabwe."

They applauded me.

By ten the next morning we were in the school bus on our way back to Harare.

25

I stood at the bus stop, wondering what to do with my heavy trunk. My school friends had helped me lift it down from the bus, but how was I going to carry it from the bus stop to some unknown destination?

"Why don't you leave it with me until you find someone to help you with it?" the guard at the museum gate said.

I accepted his offer gratefully.

At my sponsor's office I was given the address of two of my peers and the promise that I could collect my allowance in two days' time.

I found the address easily and knocked. The owner of the house opened the door. She was an amiable woman with a big heart. I liked her instantly. "Come in," she said. "I'm Agnes."

"Thank you," I said and introduced myself. "Could you tell me whether Garang Makuei and Angok Deng lodge here?" I then asked. "They are both from Sudan."

It had been a few months since I had seen them and I was looking forward to meeting them again. I had first met Garang Makuei in Panyido. He was always laughing and joking; a funny, sociable guy. Now he knew all the singers in Harare and some from South Africa. We called him "Man for himself" because he would vanish from our sight whenever he had money. Angok I had first met in Ifo. He had been the one boy in the camp who really struggled to fend for himself and the first to temporarily lose his eyesight as a result of malnutrition. He was a quiet gentleman who always seemed to be in control of his emotions, although we, his friends, knew how the absence of his family distressed him – the only family member he had ever known was his grandmother, and he would quickly become completely preoccupied with his memories of her if anyone happened to mention her name.

"Of course they are staying with me," Agnes said, "but right now they aren't around. They've gone on a trip with their school."

"I've just come back from boarding school and was wondering if I could move in with them for a while," I said.

"You're welcome," Agnes replied. "They've told me all about you."

Agnes took me to a room and handed me a key. She even brought me some orange juice.

It was good to know that my compatriots' good reputation had earned me free accommodation, but I still had no one to help me with my trunk.

Back at the museum the watchman helped me lift it onto my head and I staggered off, but it soon felt as if my neck would break and I had to ask a passer-by to help me lift it down again. Perspiring profusely, and with an aching neck, I eventually dragged the trunk all the way to Agnes's house.

We, the boys from Sudan, had always had a policy that worked well: what is mine is ours. So I changed into some casual clothes – black Levi's, a white T-shirt and a pair of Reeboks – that I found in the room and went out in search of acquaintances.

Having had no luck I returned to the room and spent the night there by myself, reading the boys' books.

"Don't you worry," Agnes reassured me the next day. "Your friends will be back soon and lots of other boys will drop in. You'll see."

At ten the first two visitors arrived. They were Tong Lual and

Kout Magot, two boys I had met in Harare when I was still struggling to find a school that would accept me. I was happy to see them again and we spent the morning catching up on news.

"Have you heard that Cyer is married and living in Canada?" the one asked.

"Magir Kiir is in Canada too," the other said, joining in. "You remember him? The guy who got some money from America and gave it away to people who were hungrier than himself."

"Koul Bol is still in Ifo with Madhiel Atem."

"Do you remember Marko Akec Deng from Panyido? The one who always said that our future would come through education? He trained as a teacher in Kenya and is now working with a mission in Sudan and Kenya."

Of course I remembered him! At Panyido the two of us had sworn to always be friends. We also shared the dream of being educated. He was a teacher now!

After a while we took a bus to the suburb of Waterfalls, where we found seventeen Sudanese boys gathered in a compound. Their landlord was as friendly as Agnes had been. "Be free. I enjoy your company," he said.

Four of us had just sat our Zimbabwean National Certificate and the others clubbed together to buy some food to celebrate the event. We ate and drank and played chess and card games until the small hours.

Then, as usual, the conversation turned to social issues and to our SPLA representative in Harare:

"How come we are locked out of the SPLA offices again?"

"Dr Benjamin spurns us and uses us at the same time."

"We'd better be careful. Let's not antagonise the Zimbabwean government. If we use violence we'll become targets."

135

"Yes, let's rather spend our time finding out all we can about the doctor's career."

"He's a politician, jijamer. Politicians don't acknowledge their faults. They declare war!"

"What we need is a government office that will back us."

* * *

The next day was a busy one. Garang Makuei was back and I went with him to Agnes's place and moved in. I also collected my allowance.

It was the Christmas season and we were restless. A group of homeless boys broke Dr Benjamin's gate and moved into the SPLA building.

Curious to find out how he would react this time, we paid them a visit. And there we found Dr Benjamin himself – in the capacity of barman! He had turned the reception area into a nightclub and was serving drinks to a glittering crowd of ambassadors and other VIPs.

A number of Sudanese boys were mingling with the guests. Dr Benjamin had called the police in an effort to have them evicted, they gleefully told us, but the officers had merely said, "How are we supposed to know who your guests are? How are we to identify your enemies? You welcome the Arabs we have been ordered to protect you from and you want us to chuck out your own countrymen. We'd better report this to our boss."

So while Dr Benjamin was entertaining his guests a growing number of boys were making their beds in every corner of the building. When, at last, the party was over our representative carried what he called his "private documents" – a file full of seemingly meaningless papers – into the main office and locked the door.

This situation continued night after night until Dr Benjamin gained the assistance of some high-ranking police authority. However, by then the police officers at the gate were our friends and we had an arrangement with them to let us enter when the representative wasn't looking. And Martin Malou, who worked for Dr Benjamin, would also smuggle us in.

Around this time a rumour started to circulate that the representative was so mean that he denied even his own relatives accommodation. Whatever the truth of this statement, we knew plenty of people who had fallen foul of the representative. A woman called Rose Nyewar Chol, whose husband had been killed in an attempted coup, had fled to Harare with her four children. She had pleaded with Dr Benjamin for assistance, but he had turned a deaf ear. Machok, a war veteran who had lost a hand and was trying to survive with a young son, was another of our acquaintances who was refused shelter. He had no choice but to put the little boy in an orphanage and return to the front line.

In the end it was frustration that caused the young Sudanese to explode. We believed that the only escape from our misery was through education and the representative was thwarting every effort we made.

One evening, a group of boys again mingled with the guests in Dr Benjamin's nightclub. At closing time, when the other guests had gone, they started an argument with the representative and his assistant barman about the R & B music they wanted to listen to. Three of my friends and I were in another part of the building. We heard the raised voices. Then there was a shattering of glasses and a crashing of furniture. We later learned that some boys had threatened to beat up Dr Benjamin and his barman, but had been prevented by the others in the same group.

That night it was the quiet Angok who took control of our little group. He rushed to the door, locked it and hid the key. We were eager to join the fray, but Angok kept appealing to us to calm down. "Please, guys! Stay here! Don't hit *me*! Remember, what they are destroying is ours. We have nowhere else to go. Who knows, Dr Benjamin may soon be replaced by someone else, but we'll still be here."

His words may have been wise, but I must admit that if it hadn't been for the locked door and the fact that the window was too small for me to crawl through I would have been in the bar, fighting.

It was five o'clock in the morning when the boys allowed the representative and his assistant to leave. The bar was a wreck and the boys were appalled when they realised what they had done. They could only wait for the police to arrive.

Twenty minutes later, the officer whose task it was to guard the SPLA offices stopped his car outside the building with its blue lights flashing. He came into the building and found the boys huddled inside. "Enough is enough!" he warned them. "Don't ever do anything like this again! These offices are now under government management and you'll have to leave. I understand why you boys have done this. We have heard your voice. But we can't condone violence."

We were greatly relieved. But, four days later, three boys – Bol Bol, Makur Majok and my great friend Chol Biem – were arrested at the gate of the SPLA offices. It was a Friday and so they spent three days in jail before they were allowed to apply for bail. Another six boys, myself included, were summoned to report to the police station, where we were informed that the barman had pressed charges against us. The barman, not the representative!

Dr Benjamin must have realised how much embarrassment a trial would have caused him and he had persuaded the barman to press charges instead. Fortunately, the case was soon withdrawn.

* * *

Then the new millennium arrived and, with it, new opportunities!

I had obtained my Form IV certificate, but there was so much more to learn. Our sponsor announced that in 2000 only students in Forms I, II and III would be sponsored; those who had finished high school would have to find a way to earn a living. I was overcome with anxiety. I would have to leave Zimbabwe, I thought. But where could I go? Certainly not back to Sudan! I recalled Dr Benjamin's words: "Go back to Sudan, boys, and join the army. We have automatic guns now. We need people like you, people who know English, to fire them and kill our enemies."

That would be the final failure! I could not return as Dr Benjamin's soldier, serving politicians like him who were lining their pockets with the money they were busy begging from the world on behalf of the poor Sudanese they claimed to represent.

What I really yearned to do was to enrol at Space College – a splendid institution that offered quality education – for a course in Public Relations. They were accredited by the University of Zimbabwe and had their main campus on Takawira Street in Harare.

Jok Mading Deng, who had a job as a relief director in Harare, came to my rescue. I had met Jok one long weekend when I was sitting on the lawn under a tree in the SPLA garden with some friends. We saw a white Toyota come through the gates and a man get out of it. He seemed to be Sudanese, but he was shorter, and his complexion lighter than most Sudanese men. We were curious, so we followed him into the offices. His father was Sudanese, he told us, and his mother American. Soon we were all chatting like old friends, exchanging experiences. After a while he called me to the main entrance for a private talk. "I'd like to be your friend," he said.

When, in desperation, I turned to Jok for assistance, he gave me sufficient money to pay my fees and a little extra for three months' accommodation.

26

It was 2002 and I had made up my mind to leave Harare as soon as I had finished my Public Relations course at Space College. Luckily, I was allowed to sit my final examinations in April even though I had not settled my account in full. Unfortunately, afterwards, I was informed that I would not receive my certificate until I had paid the outstanding amount, plus interest.

God helped me. On 25 April He brought a Sudanese visitor to the house I was staying in. Towongo Leonard was a newcomer to Harare. Short, muscular and obviously quite clever, he wanted me to show him the city and tell him about life in Zimbabwe. "Santino," he said, "if things are really so bad, if you are starving, why are you still here?"

"I *want* to go to South Africa," I told him, "but I can't leave until I have paid the amount I still owe my school."

I was showing Towongo the sights of Harare – I remember we were between the cathedral and the supreme court, those two magnificent stone buildings – when he stopped abruptly and looked at me. "I have been thinking about your situation, Santino," he said. "It's so much like my own. I thought, at first, that you were going to ask me for money to pay your debts and travel to South Africa, but you didn't. Perhaps, in your heart of hearts, you long to return to Sudan instead and look for your parents?" When I did not reply, he continued, "But South Africa may be a better option, after all. Why don't we go together? If you agree, I'll give you enough money to pay your school what you owe them and buy a bus ticket. Reimburse me when you are able to. Okay?"

I was puzzled. Did he really mean what he said?

As if to answer my question, he gave me fifty US dollars right there and promised me more.

Would I ever be in a position to help others in the way so many people had helped me? I wondered. When that day came, I swore, I would remember the lessons they had taught me.

The next morning I exchanged my US dollars for Zim dollars and went to settle my account at Space College. It had already been transferred to their lawyers, they said, but they allowed me to pay anyway. I left the school a free man. Thanks to Towongo Leonard I now no longer had any unfinished business in Harare.

What now remained of Towongo's money would have to get both of us to South Africa. He put me in charge of the budget. We converted a hundred US dollars into South African rand and a hundred US dollars into Zim dollars, and on 27 April we took a train to Mutare. From there we took a bus to Chipinge, where we stayed in a refugee camp. Finally, early on 1 May, we boarded a bus for Beit Bridge and South Africa.

We arrived at the border at five o'clock in the afternoon. We were both rather nervous about crossing the border without travel documents and I was relieved when we ran into Daniel Panther, a boy I knew from Panyido. He too was hoping to get into South Africa and was happy to join us.

In no time at all we found ourselves surrounded by strangers clamouring for the job of escorting us across the Limpopo River illegally. There was something about them that made us wary so we approached three other gentlemen instead and explained to them that we needed to cross the border that night as we couldn't afford to pay for a hotel room. "It will cost you a hundred US dollars each," they informed us.

"That's too much," I protested. "But thanks, we'll try elsewhere. Sorry for troubling you."

"How much do you have in Zim dollars?" one of them asked.

"Six thousand," I said.

"Make it ten."

We knocked them down to seven thousand and agreed to pay once we had safely crossed the river.

There were three of them and three of us. Which group would be the stronger in case of trouble? I wondered. Could we trust them? Did they trust us? They had a cellphone. We had money.

* * *

About an hour later we all got into a taxi that took us some distance along the border. "This is where we get out," one of our escorts said.

We clambered out of the taxi and watched it disappear down the track.

"This is the South African border," another of the men said. "You can pay us now."

But I had been told what the border was like and we had certainly not crossed it! "Take us to the taxi rank and you'll get your money," I said.

The three men advanced menacingly. It was clear that they were going to attack us.

"My friends," I warned them, "you will be very sorry if you try to rob us. We may be younger than you, but come on, let's fight like men!"

Daniel and I were ready to throw ourselves on them, but Towongo held us back. "Wait," he said, "let's talk."

The other side also had a peacemaker and he appealed to the

other two: "Hey, guys, let's treat our friends nicely. Let's take them to the South African side."

"No!" objected the one they called Baba Chipo. "It's too risky."

"All right," I said, "then there's no need for us to pay you. You haven't done your job. Why don't you go back?"

The peacemaker eventually persuaded us to pay his friends 2 000 Zim dollars for the little they had done. He himself would take us the rest of the way. "Mind you, it's dangerous," he said. "But I'll do it to help you. You can give me the five thousand dollars when we get to the other side. If you don't, I won't worry, but God will see you."

He took us to the top of a hill and showed us where the border really was. Then he pointed out the border post at Beit Bridge and the town of Musina.

Leaving the hill behind, we followed the course of the river for some distance, plodding silently through dry sand. The water level was low and after a while we reached a spot where we could cross the river with ease.

We were still very nervous, though. The handles on Towongo's bag were squeaking under its weight. "Let me carry it for you," I whispered. "I know how to hold it."

That night we put our trust in our guide, following where he led – I walked directly behind him, then came Daniel and Towongo brought up the rear.

It took us about an hour to reach the fence near Musina. "We'd better check the security situation first," whispered our guide. "You," he said, talking to me, "come with me."

Daniel and Towongo, meanwhile, were to hide in the bush.

We made our way slowly towards the fence, but just as we came close enough to touch it we saw a police car approaching.

We fell flat, covered ourselves with sand and waited, hardly breathing, until the car had gone.

Digging a tunnel in the hard earth under the security fence with our bare hands was hard work. I was the first to put my head into the hole and drag my body through. Then I ran for cover. Our guide came next, followed by Towongo and, finally, by Daniel.

"The Beit Bridge filling station is not far from here," our guide told us, pointing. "From there you can walk to the main road and take a minibus taxi to Pretoria."

"Great! Thank you very much," I said, handing him the agreed amount.

"Thank you," he said, "but there's another fence, just like this one, and you will have to dig another hole. That is, unless you'd prefer to crawl through those wires over there. It's easier, but then you'll have to follow the dirt road to the main road and there are often police vehicles on it."

"I'd rather face the police than more digging," I said and my friends agreed.

We slipped through the wires and somehow managed to escape the watchful eyes of the South African police as we made our way towards Beit Bridge. However, when we attempted to hitch a ride on the main road the drivers of passing taxis and trucks didn't seem to notice us either. The only place where we would be able to board a taxi, we realised, was at the border gate.

"We'd better split up as soon as we reach that line of trucks," I suggested as we approached the gate. "Three boys walking together will look suspicious."

I went first. A big mama had just got out of a truck and was on her way to the gate, so I just pretended to be with her. Daniel came next, followed by Towongo. Then I heard a commotion behind me and Towongo called out. Turning round, I saw him surrounded by men who seemed to be members of a gang. Daniel and I went to his rescue. "Why are you holding this boy?" I asked.

"You're illegal. Bribe me and I'll let him go," one of the gang members said.

"We aren't illegal! You have no right to do this to us. Come on, boys, let's go," I said, picking up Towongo's bag.

As Daniel and I walked off we could hear Towongo begging the gang to let him go. We didn't look back.

"Hey, you! Come here!" two policemen called out to us as we walked past. "Let's see your passports."

"We can show you our SPLA membership cards, sir," I said. "They are our passports. We are on our way from Johannesburg to Harare."

"Your SPLA cards may not get you there," one of the officers said. "You'd better sleep on the South African side tonight and try again tomorrow. If you really are from Sudan it will be okay, but watch out, there are many strangers around. You can't trust them."

Wow! It was good to be looked after by the South African police!

"I'd better go and look for Towongo," I told Daniel when the officers had returned to their duties. "Will you stay here with our bags?"

It wasn't long before I bumped into two of the gang members who had caught Towongo. "Where's my brother, guys?" I asked them nicely.

"Buy us a beer and we'll tell you," the one gang member said.

"Okay, but first show me where he is," I replied.

"This is South Africa," the other gang member said angrily, "and not the fucking country you come from!"

146

"I know, but this *is* Africa, and not long ago you were fighting a war like my country is doing now," I countered, trying to calm him down. "My problems are your problems."

They laughed. "Okay," said the one who had spoken first. "Just give us something for bread."

I gave them 500 Zim dollars and we shook hands.

"Your friend has taken a taxi to Musina," they told me.

So Daniel and I boarded another minibus taxi and left for Pretoria. I had hardly any money left, but Daniel still had twenty US dollars.

* * *

At midnight our taxi stopped at a police blockade. There were eighteen passengers in the taxi. All passports were collected and handed to a police officer. Daniel and I offered our SPLA membership cards and were called out to explain. "Where are you from?" the officer wanted to know.

"From southern Sudan, sir," we replied.

"Do you intend to apply for asylum in South Africa?" he asked.

"Yes, sir."

"Then there's no problem. Have a nice trip."

All was well! We could just sit back and relax.

* * *

At five o'clock in the morning, after travelling all night, the driver dropped us on a street that was already quite busy. "This is Pretoria, guys," he said, as early-morning commuters rushed past us on their way to work.

"We need to get to the city centre," I told Daniel. "Wait for me. I'll find out if there's a bus."

We had both heard of South Africa's soaring crime rate and

I was worried about asking anyone for assistance. Eventually, I approached an elderly man who looked fairly harmless and he directed me to the right bus stop.

We boarded a bus and took a seat, expecting a conductor to come and collect our fares. All the other passengers had tickets that they had shown to the driver as they had climbed on to the bus, but there was no conductor. However, there was a preacher – a short man in a black shirt – who stood up and delivered a sermon. When he had finished, he sat down, near me. He must be a man of God, I thought. It would be safe to speak to him. "Excuse me, sir. Is this bus going to the city centre?" I asked.

"Yes."

"Do you know where the UNHCR offices are?"

"UNHCR?" he said. "I'm sorry, I'm not sure."

He repeated the question to a lady sitting near us. She happened to know where the UN Information Centre was and they wrote the address down on a piece of paper for me. "The next stop is mine," the preacher said. "Get off when I do and I'll give you directions."

We did as he suggested and Daniel and I followed his directions – down Schoeman Street as far as Prinsloo Street – until we saw *UN Information Centre* written in huge letters on a wall. The door was open and a security guard was standing in the lobby. "Are these the UNHCR offices, sir?" we asked.

"Yes. Are you newcomers?"

"Yes, sir."

"Then you'd better go to Home Affairs first," he said. "That's where you are supposed to report." He gave us the address.

By this time Daniel and I were starving. There was a café on the corner, so we spent twenty rand on some buns and cooldrinks and sat down to celebrate our safe arrival in Pretoria. As we were leaving the café we bumped into Santo, a Sudanese friend of ours from Harare. Many of the guys we knew had moved to Johannesburg, he told us, but some were still in Pretoria, though he wasn't exactly sure where. He himself was staying with Awang. He then accompanied us to Home Affairs, where I joined a long queue.

Halfway down the line a woman asked me what I was doing there. "You're in the wrong building," she told me after I had explained my situation. "Home Affairs has another building where they deal with refugees." And she gave me complicated directions to an address some kilometres away.

I rejoined Daniel and Santo, but by the time I had explained to them what the lady had told me I had forgotten which way to turn. Fortunately, a fruit vendor outside the building pointed us in the right direction and we found the place.

There were crowds of refugees waiting outside the building. Some had been waiting for many days, I gathered. Awang was there too. He had come to see an official about his permit. We embraced and I introduced him to Daniel. It was so good to see Awang again, my friend Awang who had been with me the day I was bitten by the police dog in Harare. "If you have only just arrived," he told us, "I'd better take you to Lawyers for Human Rights first. They can give you protection papers. If you stay here you'll wait forever and be harassed by the police."

I was learning fast. Apparently the South African police objected to refugees moving through the streets in groups, so we split up. Daniel and Awang went ahead and Santo and I followed. At the lawyers' offices our two friends excused themselves, promising to call for us later.

We had just taken a seat when I heard another distinctly Sudanese voice: "Hi, jijamer! How are you doing?"

It was Bilal Sam. He and Sixtus Mabok were there for a meeting. I hadn't met them before, but they were from Sudan. We were brothers. "You're lucky," Bilal said. "You won't have to sleep on the streets tonight, like we did when we arrived. When you've seen the lawyer, wait for us and we'll take you back to our place."

While Bilal and Sixtus were busy with their meeting, a helpful lawyer handed us our protection papers and directed us to the offices of the Jesuit Refugee Services where, he told us, we could apply for financial assistance. After he had finished his meeting Bilal accompanied us.

But at the JRS offices the official was not sure whether he would be able to assist us. "Come back tomorrow," he said. "If we can find the money we'll help you."

We spent the night at Bilal's place. The landlord wasn't keen on more Sudanese boys moving in, and it must have taken hard work on the part of Bilal, Sixtus and their roommate, Mike, to persuade him to let us stay for a month.

* * *

The following day, after a fax from Lawyers for Human Rights, the JRS was more accommodating. When Daniel and I returned they promised to let us have 230 rand per month each for food and accommodation. Another acquaintance of ours, Peter Bior Deng, and a few others contributed as much as they could, and we were soon the proud owners of a bed and a blanket each. I could reimburse them as soon as I had paid my debt to Towongo, they said.

Towongo! I still had his bag! We were convinced that he had to be in South Africa – there was no way he would have returned to Zimbabwe – so Bilal called some friends of his in Johannesburg.

Towongo was there, worrying about us, they said. He had seen us being arrested by the police and fled! But he would be coming to Pretoria soon to see Lawyers for Human Rights and JRS. When he did, we met him at the JRS offices. With him was Chol, a relative of Daniel's. I was particularly happy to see Towongo again and Daniel was overjoyed to see his cousin Chol. They had been together in Kenya, but last he had heard Chol was in prison somewhere in Mozambique.

We took Towongo and Chol to our friends' place, but by now there were eleven of us crowded into two rooms, which created considerable tension. We made up our minds to find our own accommodation at the end of the month. Meanwhile, we spent all the time we could on the street.

As soon as I could I gave Towongo as much money as I was able to. "Thanks for the loan," I said. "I'll try to give you the balance next month."

He hugged me. "I'm the one who should be grateful. You have helped me in so many ways. I never thought you would be able to repay the money so soon. Okay, if you give me another hundred rand next month, to make it up to a hundred US dollars, we'll forget about the rest."

I promised to do exactly that.

* * *

On 10 May we were taken to Home Affairs by a lawyer from Lawyers for Human Rights to collect our permits. We were called in for interviews, had our photos taken, and after lunch (paid for by a Home Affairs official) we signed for our temporary permits, which were valid for one month.

By now it was high time that Daniel, Chol and I moved out of our friends' crowded rooms. Bilal, Sixtus and Mike were already in trouble with their roommates for letting us sleep there. Daniel and I were unable to rent a room for ourselves, though, and Chol's application for an allowance had been turned down by the JRS, as he was now too old to qualify as an "unaccompanied minor". Daniel and Chol spent a day in the city centre looking for a suitable spot, while I hunted for a place in the densely populated suburb of Sunnyside.

After several hours of searching I was exhausted and ready to sleep anywhere. Then, looking up, I saw a light shining from Pastor Manny's chapel on the second floor of an office building.

Some days before, Pastor Manny had knocked at our door to invite us to his church. When he left, he had quietly pressed something into my hand – the day's offerings from his church! I thought I would drop in for a chat.

"Hi, Santino," he welcomed me. "How are you?"

"Fine. How are you doing?"

"Fine. Chol and Daniel tell me that you are looking for accommodation."

"Oh, have they been here?" I asked. "Do you know where I can find them?"

"They've gone to look for a place to sleep."

"Oh, okay."

We then changed the topic.

I was about to leave when Chol, Daniel and Bilal came knocking on the door. They hadn't found anywhere we could spend the night either.

"Listen, guys," the pastor said, "I'll be leaving for America in a fortnight's time. But while I'm still here, I would like you to come and stay with me. Bilal, you can come too. Okay?"

We were speechless. God must have seen us running up and down the streets all day.

Pastor Manny finished his work in the chapel and we got into his car. We stopped at Bilal's place to collect our blankets and we, who had thought that we would spend a sleepless night on a street corner, were driven to a comfortable home in Menlo Park. Conditions there were rather crowded too, but the time we spent with Pastor Manny in his house was just great. He even arranged for us to play basketball at the University of Pretoria.

27

Misericordia International Centre is located in the centre of Pretoria. It was established by a refugee for refugees and has become a gathering place for people from Sudan, the Congo, Rwanda, Burundi, Angola and other war-torn African countries.

For me it brought a new challenge. When I left Visitation High School in Harare a friend said: "Good luck! Go well, Santino. Remember that the first adventure you encounter is never the last. When you have climbed a hill and reached the top you will discover another, higher hill beyond it. Accept the challenge. Climb it!"

I would never have considered joining the English class at Misericordia if it hadn't been for the sense of utter meaninglessness that overwhelmed me in those early days in Pretoria. After Pastor Manny had left for America I found myself wandering aimlessly through the parks and streets. I had been granted time to live, but I had nothing to live for. I thought of the boys I had once known, now scattered all over the world, thinking of themselves as the "futureless generation" of southern Sudan. I thought of the politicians and their propaganda, of the SPLA soldiers fighting the Arabs, of my peers suffering in refugee camps in the warzone. And here I was doing nothing at all – jobless, useless, leading a meaningless life.

Meanwhile, Bilal and Sixtus were attending school. "How do you do it?" I asked them. "Who's sponsoring you?"

"Why don't you come too? We're halfway through the course, but we'll ask the teacher if she'll admit you. The JRS will pay your registration fee."

So Sixtus took me to Misericordia and introduced me to the receptionist, who in turn referred us to the teacher. She welcomed me to her class and the Jesuit Refugee Services paid the registration fee and provided me with a student card.

* * *

Attending English lessons at Misericordia came to mean a lot to us Sudanese boys. The teacher was Ma Sannie, a white Afrikaans woman who seemed to understand our situation in her country. She brought tea and biscuits to every lesson and allowed us to talk about ourselves, our views and ambitions.

She also invited us Sudanese boys to her house for lunch one Sunday. We were living very lonely lives without our parents, so it was nice to be going to someone's home.

We had been told to gather at Misericordia to be collected. Ma Sannie's sister, Rykie, a most entertaining lady, arrived first. We didn't know that our teacher had a sister, but as soon as she arrived we saw the family resemblance and chatted away happily with Rykie until Ma Sannie arrived.

Both women drove white Toyota Corollas and each car could take three boys. I went with Ma Rykie. We were headed for the suburb of Wonderboom and it was quite exciting to drive through a part of Pretoria I hadn't been to before.

Cooldrinks were served in a small green garden, after which we went in to lunch. We said grace and helped ourselves to the food. And then we talked about many things; asked questions and considered answers. Later we went to see the Wonderboom – a wild fig tree that is thought to be over a thousand years old.

It was late evening when we got home, but I still felt empty. I knew that the vacuum I felt inside me had to do with missing my parents and family. If only I could earn enough money to return to Sudan, I thought, then I could go in search of whatever had remained of my family. It was then that I decided to borrow 500 rand and start a business. I knew I could buy clothes cheaply from the wholesalers in Johannesburg and sell them again at a good price to the early-morning commuters at Wonderboom station. I was convinced that I would be able to make a profit, pay my rent, buy food and still save a little each week.

Unfortunately, although my business was successful, the permit that Home Affairs had given me prohibited work and the police kept confiscating my stock. After some weeks I was left with only 550 rand, which I deposited with Ma Sannie.

* * *

After our final examination, Ma Sannie and her sister again entertained us at her home – and this time the whole class was invited. There were two tables. At my table, Ma Rykie suggested that we tell stories to make one another laugh, but the story I really wanted to tell was a sorrowful one and while Ma Sannie was pouring the coffee I started telling her about my life and the lives of my peers in the refugee camps. She was interested, but everyone was leaving and it was a long story. "I tell you what," she suggested. "I'll pick you up next Saturday morning. We can go somewhere quiet and you can tell me your whole story."

I agreed and it was decided that she would meet me at Misericordia at ten o'clock the following Saturday.

* * *

Saturday morning found me reading a book by Victor Frankl – *Man's Search for Meaning*. I was finding it inspiring. It was like

The Magic of Thinking Big, the book that my friend from Bangladesh had lent me on the bus to Zimbabwe, and *Meditation*, a great book I had found in a library Pastor Manny had taken me to when he had come back from America.

When Ma Sannie arrived we drove to the tea garden behind Melrose House and found a quiet corner. I didn't eat much; I just wanted to talk! She had brought an atlas so that I could show her where the places I mentioned were.

My story took many hours to tell, but when I had finished she said, "So, Santino, why don't you write a book?"

I had always felt the need to tell others how politicians had turned human lives upside down in southern Sudan and Ma Sannie was not the first person to suggest that I write a book. Jok Mading Deng, my benefactor in Harare, Pastor Manny and many other friends had also suggested it, but I had never had the opportunity to do so before. This time Ma Sannie offered me the use of her computer. And that's how I began writing my book.

28

I wrote this story fast, unburdening myself of the memories that weighed so much on my mind. But when I started writing my story I didn't know how it would end. Unexpectedly, on 30 August 2002, my birthday, something happened.

I was at Bilal's place. All my best friends were there and as usual conversation turned to the whereabouts of the people we had known in different countries. I had sufficient money for a phone call to Zimbabwe, so I decided to call my friend, Garang Makuei, who was still living at Agnes's place in Harare.

"Aher!" he exclaimed as he came on the line. "Your mother is looking for you! I spoke to an uncle of yours on the phone a few days ago. His name is Riak Atem and he lives in America."

He explained that he had called some Sudanese friends of his in Las Vegas and that a man by the name of Riak Atem had answered the phone. Garang's friends were not at home, so he and Riak had had a chat instead. When Riak had told Garang that he came from my area, Twich County, Garang had mentioned my name. Riak then told him that he had had a young nephew called Aher, who had disappeared in the war and whose mother had never ceased searching for him. It was me!

"Your uncle wants you to call him," Garang said and gave me the telephone number.

As I wrote this story, I could not tell what the future held for me. But I knew that I would not rest until I had seen my mother and my father. My friends know me as Santino, but when I was born my mother called me Aher, which means "light". I have become Aher again.

PART 2

1

Little did I know that only a few weeks after I spoke to my uncle Riak Atem, in Las Vegas – a relative I never even knew existed – my long-cherished dream would come true.

As soon as they had heard my good news, some of my friends gave or lent me money. Combined with the money I had saved from my business this was enough to turn my dream into a reality, and on 17 December 2002 I found myself at Lokichokio airport in northern Kenya, on the border with Sudan. I had finally come to look for my parents who had been lost for so many years.

Before I had left South Africa I had made up my mind to remain calm. Day and night, dreams of my mother and father had haunted me and I knew that I couldn't allow myself to imagine what would happen when I met my parents, it would be too much. Instead, I tried to concentrate all my energy on boarding the plane that would take me home, to the place where my history began – the town of Turalei in the Bahr el Ghazal region.

At Lokichokio I bought a ticket for 300 US dollars. My flight was scheduled for 21 December. On that day I would be reunited with the parents I did not remember. On that day I would meet my history. I would find my home.

Lokichokio was not new to me. I had been there in 1992 when, with thousands of other refugees, I had been pushed over the border into the UNHCR camp of Kakuma. Fascinated, I went off to look for the place where I had once lived. It was still just as dry and windy as I remembered it. Loki had changed, though. It was better developed and planes of all kinds were parked on the tarmac, waiting to fly relief operations into Sudan or to return to Nairobi.

The days passed slowly. My flight was to be the last one into Sudan before the charter company suspended operations for the Christmas season. Of course, I was concerned. What if they cancelled the flight?

* * *

The morning of 20 December arrived. My fellow passengers and I waited anxiously for the flight operators to collect our luggage for loading. We were due to depart at six the next morning and our bags had to be loaded the day before.

When the car left with the luggage, I returned to my hotel room and lay down, facing the ceiling. I was relieved that my luggage was on its way to the plane; I was feeling very light, weightless almost. Was it true that I was going back to the place of my birth? I asked myself. How would I greet the people waiting at the airstrip when we landed? No one would know me and I wouldn't know anyone. Would I be able to introduce myself to them? How would I enquire about my parents?

Suppose they didn't know my parents? I suddenly thought. Or confronted me with the unthinkable news that they had passed away or were no longer living in the area? The war had scattered people beyond the borders of Sudan! What would I do? Or if I did meet my mother and my father, how would I, their lost son, approach them? How would I show them my true feelings, tell them how much I had missed them? It had been fifteen years, my whole life!

My brain was at war! I had thought I'd take a nap, but I was unable to sleep. I couldn't clear my mind of memories and there were no answers to the endless questions in my head.

I got up and rinsed my face with water from the tap, then returned to my room to admire the clothes I had selected to wear the next day. Passing through Zimbabwe, I had picked items a journalist or tourist might wear. The outfit was smart, but would also allow me to mingle with the crowd once I disembarked in Sudan. What I liked best was that my windbreaker had a hood that could hide my face whenever I didn't want to be noticed.

The 20 December was a difficult, endless day. I had no company, no one to chat to, so I went for a walk, but nothing I saw made any sense to me. I couldn't understand myself.

Back from the walk, I had supper at the hotel, took a bath and went to my room. I told myself that I would keep calm the next day and not rush into anything – regardless of whether things turned out to be good or bad.

At last I drifted into a deep, dreamless sleep.

* * *

By daybreak I was awake and dressed. I joined the other passengers in a nearby hotel from which we were to be collected by the airline's car. The car arrived and dropped us at the security checkpoint. Our documents were checked and we were allowed to proceed to the plane.

I kept telling myself that there was nothing unusual about this trip, that nothing was new – even though I *was* on my way to the place of my birth, to my parents I had missed so much for fifteen years, whose whereabouts I had only recently discovered. But I was still afraid: afraid of talking to people, afraid of being disappointed, afraid of being a victim of happiness.

I stared at the pilots as they headed towards the cockpit. They seemed so distinguished, so different, unlike anyone I had ever seen before. They instructed us to board, to locate our seats and to fasten our seatbelts.

The plane started moving, faster and faster. I covered my wristwatch with my right hand. I would wait until the moment we took off before I checked the time. Then the front wheel left the tarmac. We were airborne! I glanced at my watch. It was 07:17 sharp, and in a moment I would be flying over the border and into Sudan – heading towards my long-lost parents. It was a moment of great adventure!

I had crossed Sudan on foot and now I was about to see what the country looked like from the air. The plane circled Loki, then turned towards the border. Through the clouds I could see how different the buildings in Loki town looked from the manyatta – the traditional Turkana huts – on the outskirts.

Sudan and Kenya, two nations divided by a great range of mountains! But in our little plane it took us no more than three minutes to pass over the mountains and see the rocky earth give way to savanna. This was southern Sudan as I remembered it.

As the plane gained altitude, I was fascinated by the view. And the clouds! There were huge clouds above us and below us. We entered one – suddenly there was nothing but white mist enveloping us – only to emerge again into clear blue sky. But there were things I needed to know before we landed at Rumbek, our first stop, so I turned to the passenger sitting next to me. "Is this the first time you have flown over this area?" I enquired.

"I've done it at least five times," he replied.

"Then you will be able to tell me if we are going to fly over the Nile?"

"Of course," he said, "the Nile and some other great rivers. In thirty minutes or so the weather will clear and you will be able to see much better. It is only around Loki that it is always so cloudy."

He was soon proved right. The clouds vanished and the blue Sudanese sky was the best there ever was. We were flying very high now, but I could distinguish smoke rising and, of course, rivers. "Is that the Nile?" I kept asking, but every time my fellow passenger just shook his head. "The Nile is much wider. I'll tell you when we get to it," he assured me.

At last the Nile did appear below us, but I found it hard to distinguish between the main channel and its many tributaries – where the water met and where it parted again. The river was so wide and so long!

When we touched down at Rumbek I checked my watch again. It was 09:37. The passengers alighted, goods were unloaded and the plane took on fuel.

I was delighted to touch the soil of Sudan once again. The sight of Rumbek gave me courage to face my circumstances. I had actually arrived in Sudan, the land of my birth. No one was in a hurry, so I went to the restroom, then I found a seat near the plane and waited for our flight to resume.

Our next stop was Mapel, where we spent only a few minutes before we headed for Malual Kun. From there it was a short flight to Turalei – my destination. I cherished the time I spent at each of the towns, but the reason for my being there kept troubling me. What awaited me at Turalei? I asked myself again and again, and every time I did so fear gripped my heart.

2

Home sweet home, people say, but have they ever experienced the pain of being a stranger in what you have always considered to be your homeland?

The plane had landed and the door was open. Officials were waiting to receive the visitors to their country. Parents, relatives and friends were ready to embrace their own. But Aher Arop, big stranger and fearful man, remained in his seat, shy and anxious. Eventually, when the attendants reboarded the plane to remove the luggage, I had to stand up to identify mine. "This is our last stop," the pilot said. "Aren't you disembarking here?"

"Yes, sir. I am."

"Are you new to the area?" one of the other attendants asked.

"Yes."

I didn't know what to do. So, staying inside, I started handing the luggage to the attendant by the door. But I couldn't keep on doing that forever. Soon there were no more bags left and I had to jump down. As I busied myself with my own luggage on the tarmac inquisitive strangers approached and offered their assistance, but I covered my head with my hood.

A very tall, smart-looking gentleman who seemed to be in charge of everything on the airstrip then approached. "Are you from Nairobi?" he enquired.

"Yes, sir."

"Do you require any assistance? Do you know where to go?"

I looked up at him. "Do you know a lady called Aker Bol?" I asked. "She lives hereabouts."

"Yes, of course. Her home is just opposite this building. Would you like us to call her for you?"

"I'd appreciate it if someone could take me to her place, sir. Will my luggage be safe if I leave it here?"

"Of course. And relax, boy. This is home."

A number of people had gathered around us. They were curious to know who I was and why I had come. "Don't mind me," I said. "I am one of the boys of this town. You will know more about me when I return to collect my luggage."

One of them volunteered to take me to Aker Bol's house. He kept fishing for information, but I didn't respond.

When we got to the compound I remained behind in the yard as my guide went up to the door and knocked. A woman came to the door. "You've got a visitor outside," he told her.

Long ago, when I had arrived with my uncle at Panyido in Ethiopia, Aker, a close relative of my mother's, was among the refugees. Although the authorities wouldn't allow me to spend much time with her, my uncle Atem kept reminding me that she was a relative. However, by the time Atem was forced to join the SPLA, Aker had disappeared. I never saw her again. When we had fled the fighting in Ethiopia, I had searched for her in the women's communities, but was told that she had found her way back home, back to the town of Turalei.

I had counted on finding her still at Turalei and here she was! I was standing in her compound!

At first Aker didn't recognise me. She approached cautiously, trying to identify her unexpected guest, but I knew at once that she was Aker, my aunt. I wanted to run to her, but restrained myself. I would wait in silence, as I had planned, and present myself as an honourable man.

Aker came closer, but did not extend a hand to greet me. Then she said quietly, "Boy, may I know who you are?"

I smiled. "Who do you think I am?" I asked. "Haven't you met me before?"

She scrutinised my face, obviously wondering who could have come to visit her from another country.

"Let me guess . . . Are you Aher Dot Ajok?" she asked tentatively, using my mother's family name.

"Yes, I am," I said, grinning broadly.

My aunt grabbed me and hugged me. She was elated. "Ooh! My sister's son! I can't believe that God has brought us together again! What joy you have brought me, Aher! Please come in."

Holding me close to her, she led me into her house. I kept quiet while she was pouring out her happiness. "God is great!" she cried as soon as we were inside. "Your mother was here, in my house, only two days ago. She has always blamed me bitterly for not bringing you back to her when I returned from Panyido. She thinks I must hate her to do such a thing to her. And here you are! God has restored her lost son to her!"

"How far is my mother's village from here?" I asked.

"Not far. Four hours, maybe," she said. "But it will be dark soon. Spend the night here and tomorrow I will take you to them myself."

It was broad daylight! I couldn't possibly sleep in Turalei with my mother only a few hours away. Even if it meant walking all night it would be better than spending a sleepless night at my aunt's house.

Aker understood. "Sure, I can imagine how you must feel about your mother, but I have a baby and I'm breast-feeding, so I won't be able to go with you today. But wait, your father will be in town today, I think. He was coming for a court case. They expect a judgement today. Give me a few minutes to find out whether he's in town. If he isn't, I'll look for someone to accompany you to your village. Sit down and I'll sort things out for you."

Before she left, I begged my aunt not to spread the news of my arrival until I had been reunited with my parents and the rest of the family. I didn't want them to learn of my return from any mouth but my own. She understood and promised to keep the information to herself.

Aker soon returned with the news that my father was not yet in town. However, she had found me a guide to take me to Marol Amiol, the village where my parents lived. She hadn't told him anything, she reassured me, just the name of the village. "Once you reach the area, you can send him back and find your own way to Dot's compound," she told me. "Don't tell anyone you're her son. Just say you're a visitor."

My guide and I left straight away. "How long will it take us to get to Marol Amiol?" I asked as we set out.

"We should be there no later than nine o'clock," he replied.

"How far will we be following this path?"

"All the way until we get to the river. There we turn left. There's a boat that'll take us across to Marol Amiol."

"Will there be any problems when it gets dark?" I asked. "Bandits or wild animals?"

"Don't worry. This path is always busy, even late at night. We'll be safe."

Hearing this, I begged him to turn back and leave me to find my own way. I removed one of the T-shirts I was wearing and gave it to him, thanking him for his understanding and help.

"I can't just leave you," he protested. "What shall I tell Aker?"

"Don't worry about me," I said and started running. When I looked back he was still standing there.

I was finally on my way to meet my mother and father. They were alive and I was back, alive, to join them. I was the happiest man in Sudan that day, thanking God in my heart for the miraculous way in which He had brought me home after fifteen parentless years. I was running along, delighted, like a child playing with his mother.

* * *

I kept running and walking for an hour, pulling my hood over my face every time I encountered groups of villagers on the busy path. Then an old man appeared. He was alone, carrying a small bag on his back, a walking stick across his shoulders.

There was something vaguely, disconcertingly, familiar about him. I stared at him – his face, his gait – then approached him. I held out my hand, and he took it. "Do you know a man by the name of Arop Bol?" I asked.

"I am Arop Bol," he said, confusion on his face.

I turned away and burst out laughing. I was so proud. So happy.

But the old man was irritated and suspicious. "Why do you want to know, young man? Who are you? What are you laughing at?" he said crossly.

How could I explain to him who I was? "Haven't you met me before?" I asked, unable to hide my happy smile. "Don't I look like someone you know?"

"No, I don't know you," my father said curtly. "Who are you?"

"Do you know anyone called Aher?"

"Aher who?"

"Aher Arop Bol."

My father gazed at me in astonishment, searching my smiling face. He took a hasty step towards me, but then, before he could catch hold of me, he collapsed, dropping his bag and stick. And there he lay on the ground, clutching the earth and crying in a loud voice, which faded as he lost consciousness.

I rushed forward and turned him onto his back, frantically trying to recall my first-aid lessons as I tried to resuscitate him. A couple of passers-by offered help and we carried him to a shady spot. They wanted to know what had caused the old man to faint, but how could I explain to them what had happened without revealing my identity? "I'm sure he'll be okay," I assured them.

"I'm all right," my father told the bystanders when he came to. "Let me rest for a while. This boy will take care of me."

For a long time he just sat there, eyes downcast, holding my hand tightly to his chest. When at last he felt strong enough to get up, he embraced me – proudly, happily, patting my head and laughing. I hugged him tightly in return.

"My son, Aher! How did you recognise me when I did not know you?" he eventually asked. "When I lost you, my son, you were a very young boy who didn't even know himself, too young to have memories of your home. You couldn't count to two in your mother tongue. Yet you recognised me without anyone pointing me out to you. How did you do that, my son?"

I didn't know what to say so I just smiled at him.

"Please don't look at me. And don't smile like that!" he pleaded as I studied his face. "It's not right. You caught me by surprise. The shock could have killed me. *I* was strong enough to withstand the shock, but imagine what might have happened if you had confronted a weaker person, like your mother, like that! None of us ever expected to see you again. We haven't heard anything from you in such a very long time! You may cause someone's death! Please stop smiling at me, my son. Try to look serious, pretend that you are not happy or you may spoil everything."

When I stumbled on my father that day he had been on his way to Turalei to attend the judgement on a court case that he had hoped to win. But meeting his son was of greater importance. We picked up his stick and bag and he turned back to Marol Amiol with me. Together we headed home.

3

Around half past five we came to a small market square. My father turned to me. "Look, my son, these people know me and they are aware of the reason I was on my way to Turalei today. It would be unfair of me not to tell them why I have turned back. I'll have to buy them a drink and tell them my good news, so that tomorrow they can inform the judge why I won't be able to attend the judgement. I want you to carry on past the market. Walk slowly and I'll catch up with you."

I pulled the hood over my head and did as I was told.

When my father joined me again he took my hand and held it to express his joy. He, too, was smiling now. We continued on our way, unhurriedly.

Dusk was falling when we got to the river and my father halted. "Listen to what I'm going to tell you, Aher," he urged me. "We are very close to home. If it weren't so dark you'd be able to see our compound. But we'd better wait. No one is expecting you and your arrival is bound to cause shock. Tomorrow, once they have received word of your presence, I'll take you to meet them."

I agreed – we were father and son, after all – and we turned right towards Wunrock Adiang, the area my mother had originally come from, instead of turning left towards the river and our compound.

It was completely dark by the time we approached a large compound. "This is where we'll sleep over," my father told me. "You must be exhausted. I'm sorry I can't take you home."

"That's all right, Father," I said. "You know what's best for the family."

My father knocked at the door and I stood back, watching from the darkness as he talked to the person who came to see who was at the door.

We were offered a place to sleep and some food, but I couldn't eat. My first meal would be the one my mother prepared for me, I vowed. So I had a drink of water and got under the mosquito net. How good it was to be able just to relax!

* * *

My father woke me at five the next morning and informed the owner of the house that we were leaving. I later learned that we had spent the night at the house of Aker Bol's father.

We resumed our journey, heading back towards the river and Marol Amiol, where we hoped to find the rest of the family.

We had crossed the river and were walking through a fairly densely populated area when my father drew my attention to a particular village. "That is where your mother was born," he told me. "Her family still lives there. Your grandmother too. She is still alive, although she is blind and can no longer move about without assistance."

My grandmother! Still alive! "Please, Father, can we stop there so that you can introduce me to her?" I asked him.

"Of course," my father said, sounding serious. "It is my duty to inform your grandmother that God and the great ancestors have brought you back alive to us after so many years."

I was overwhelmed. "God is great," I exclaimed, "to give me a grandmother even before I have met my mother! But I don't want to take my grandmother by surprise like I did you. What shall we do?"

"Nobody in that compound will recognise you. They will welcome us even though they won't know you. Just remain quiet and act normally until I've found a way to tell them that God has returned you to us."

As we approached the village I begged my father to let me go on ahead on my own.

"We could do that," he replied, "but you won't know which hut is your grandmother's."

"Describe it to me, Father, please," I asked him. "Tell me how to recognise it."

"All right," he agreed. "You will see a big tree with three huts around it. That is where she lives."

I increased my pace, leaving my father to follow in my footsteps, and soon came upon the three huts.

It was a cold morning and my grandmother was sitting on a mat in the middle of the compound, enjoying the weak sunshine. There were others too – four girls pounding grain outside the kitchen and three women busy with their make-up. Acutely aware of the eyes on me, I walked up to the old woman on the mat. I sat down next to her and quietly put my hand on her shoulder. I was filled with joy and compassion. "Who are you?" my grandmother asked, and when I remained silent she appealed to the others to tell her, but they were mystified, clearly wondering what relation I could possibly be to the old lady. Then, in her friendly way, she tried to guess who I might be, calling out the names of neighbours and loved ones. "No, Grandma," the women responded after each of her guesses, "none of the names you've mentioned."

"Please help me," she begged me. "You know I can't see. How can you expect me to recognise you?"

Just then my father arrived. As is custom, he stopped some distance from the huts and waited to be greeted. I was proud of the way he observed Dinka tradition, but his glance reminded me of his admonition not to smile when I met the family.

My aunt, the one taking care of my grandmother, stood up and addressed him respectfully and the women stood up to bow to him in greeting, as is traditional. My grandmother was the only one who remained seated, but she also welcomed her son-in-law warmly and enquired after his family. My father responded humbly, assuring her that everyone was well, but his happy grin caught the attention of the other women in the compound. They looked at me with renewed interest, obviously wondering whether there was a connection between Arop Bol and the mysterious stranger who still had not removed his hand from the old woman's shoulder.

My father raised his voice: "Truly, God has brought him back to us! I met him yesterday on my way to Turalei. Don't you recognise him? He was once one of you."

"Your son, Aher, who disappeared in 1987?" one of the aunts guessed, as the others waited breathlessly for my father to reveal my identity.

"Aher!" my father responded, smiling from ear to ear.

They all rushed at me to embrace and welcome me. My grandmother burst into song, praising her great ancestors and God. She held me tight, groping for my head to kiss. "Aher Dot!" she cried. "Child of my child! Thank God and the greatest of my ancestors who have returned you to us. Neither I nor my daughter deserved the punishment of having a son disappear without a trace. And now you have been returned to us in the very month I sacrificed a bull to the ancestors! Our prayers have been answered!"

I couldn't let go of my grandmother and as my aunts, young and old, swarmed around us my father had to remind them to be gentle with the old woman. With my grandmother kissing one hand I reached out to my aunts with the other.

I had still not spoken a single word. I longed to know who these women were. Were they really aunts of mine? What were their names? I had come to meet a single relative and now there were so many. But my grandmother's songs of praise continued and I had no desire to remove my hand from her shoulder. So I merely pressed my face against her back to hide my tears. I couldn't let my father and the others see that I was crying.

My efforts to stop the tears must have caused me to gasp for breath for my grandmother now placed one hand on my chest and the other on my back to calm me. She told me to lie down with my head on her knee and asked for clean water to be brought in a calabash – the one that had never been used before, the one that had been saved for a special rite. "Don't be anxious," she soothed me. "Be calm. Don't cry. You have come home, my son."

The aunts now helped my grandmother up and handed her the calabash. Joining her in song they led her to the tomb of my grand-father and to those of all the other ancestors around the compound. She poured water from the calabash onto each grave so that the forefathers might all share in the blessing that had befallen the family. Then, finally, I was made to stand at the holy place, the great entrance to the compound, and water was poured over me and then over everyone who had witnessed this great event, from the oldest to the youngest.

After the ceremony, my grandmother and I returned to the mat. I lay down with my head on her knee and she held me, soothing me and offering me sips of water like any grandmother consoling a child. It was then that my father told them the story of how we had met.

My grandmother was surprised. "Hasn't he met his mother yet? Am I the first to see him? Before his other grandmother?" She regarded this as a great compliment, but even as she thanked my father humbly she reminded him that before any animal was slaughtered in my honour he should take me to the place where I was born – the place where my other grandmother lived and the tombs of my father's own great ancestors were. It was there that the clan elders lived and she wanted them to participate in the miracle of my return.

Being reunited with people who really cared about me was a new experience. I watched my grandmother as she held her hands high, singing joyful songs. I felt cared for and protected. It was here that I should have been all along – surrounded by family members who could have nourished me – instead of being forced to fend for myself in the wilderness for so many solitary years.

When my grandmother had finished singing she rubbed my stomach and declared that it was empty. "This child is hungry!" she told my father. "Where did you sleep last night? What did he eat?"

She sent one of my aunts to prepare some food for me and another to fetch the milk that was reserved strictly for her own use. I drank and drank until my stomach was full, with my grandmother's hand resting on it just to make sure.

At last, she called my relatives one by one to introduce them to me. They would come and sit down close to us and she would tell me their names and how we were related. Then she would explain what their obligations to me were, according to custom.

When our meal was brought, neither my grandmother nor I could eat, but we sat together, holding hands, surrounded by family. Then my grandmother resumed her singing, interpreting each of the great sacred songs for me.

Although it was wonderful to be with my grandmother and my aunts, I was now ready to head home with my father and meet the rest of the family. My grandmother was also concerned that my mother might have heard about my arrival, and, perplexed by my disappearance, be searching for me. However, I couldn't leave her home, she declared, without the blessing of a male member of the clan. Unfortunately, there were hardly any men left in the villages. Many had been killed or were still fighting as soldiers in different parts of the country – where exactly, the families didn't know. Others had taken refuge in neighbouring countries.

The sole man left to take care of clan issues in my grandmother's neighbourhood was Mayeth Nom, an old uncle. The whereabouts of only one other man were known – a son who had fled to the north of Sudan when I had run with my uncle to Ethiopia in 1987. He eventually made it to Kenya and was resettled with a group of "lost boys" in Las Vegas in America – the very uncle (not much older than myself) I had spoken to on the phone from Pretoria.

My grandmother told one of the aunts to summon Mayeth Nom to come and speak on behalf of the family. But they had already sent a messenger to his village, the aunts told her, and according to his wife he had left home that morning and would not be back until much later. They were confident, though, that he would come to acknowledge Aher Dot, even after dark.

And sure enough, in the middle of the night – while I was fast asleep in the hut where my grandmother was still singing – he arrived. Before dawn an aunt came to inform me that he was in the compound waiting to meet me. I left the hut and greeted my uncle. He spoke the great words he had come to say and I was free to leave with the blessing of my new-found family.

4

It was still dark when my father and I left my grandmother's compound, heading for Marol Amiol, the village where I belonged. It was a lovely, cool, peaceful morning, with birds calling from the trees and bushes. It was the rainy season and the new green grass growing along the narrow footpath was wet with dew.

I felt at one with nature on that great day. I was close to God and close to my ancestors. God was at work, I decided. How else could all this be possible? Through God *nothing* was impossible. He worked in mysterious and unique ways. I was actually walking with my father! How many journeys had I undertaken, how many borders had I crossed without a father to guide me? And now here he was, showing me the way home, guiding me towards the village where I belonged.

We left the forest and entered the swamp, and it was then that we saw smoke rising from a village on the bank of the river. As we emerged from the long grass and climbed to higher ground the large domed straw huts became clearly visible.

My father turned round. "Aher," he said, "do be careful with your smile, my son. You almost killed me on the day we met. Be serious. Don't even call out when you meet your mother. She is too weak to handle your coming home the way I did. But the family may have heard of your return. They may be ready to welcome you."

He had planned our approach. He wanted me to remain behind while he went ahead to prepare the way. "Remain here, under this tree," my father instructed me. "When you see me coming back, meet me halfway."

I promised to do as I was told.

Waiting under that tree was another adventure. I was filled with a sense of joyous expectation. Finally, I was to meet my mother. The void in my life was to be healed. God was at work to restore to me the love I had missed so much. But there was no picture in my memory of my mother. If she rushed towards me, surrounded by other women, how was I to recognise her?

I leaned against the tree and watched my father approaching the village. He turned towards two huts, but instead of entering either one of them he passed through the compound. He then went round two more compounds, heading for the middle one, which consisted of four thatch huts. Then he disappeared from my sight.

When he finally reappeared, alone, I started walking towards him. He waited for me at the entrance to the village. I followed him in silence, through the garden of the first compound, past the two others. Then, from inside the compound with the four huts, a woman appeared and came towards us.

"This is home, Aher," my father said, before the woman reached us. "But, before you enter, this woman will direct you to where your great ancestors are buried. Follow her."

Without a word of greeting the woman turned around and, realising how important this tradition was, I followed her. I was ready to honour my ancestors, but that didn't stop me from wondering about the whereabouts of my family. Was this woman the only person at home?

The woman led me to another large compound containing six round huts. "Stop," she said as we reached the entrance. Then she entered alone before reappearing to summon me. Inside was the tomb of my greatest ancestor. "Walk round the tomb," the woman said. "Now, step up onto it and stand up straight."

I did as I was told. Then, suddenly, a crowd of people appeared from the neighbouring huts – among them a woman I later learned was the custodian of my greatest ancestor's compound. Breaking into traditional song this woman filled an unused white calabash with water. She then asked me to step off the tomb. The first to touch me, she sprinkled water over me before using the pure water to mark my head and chest with crosses. Then she instructed me to remove my shoes and poured water over my feet.

By now the compound was filled with villagers watching the ceremony. Four or five very old men approached to fulfil their traditional role. Then some young sheep and goats were brought in and led around me by different members of the clan, who uttered spells and words of thanksgiving to God and their great ancestor for bringing me home alive.

When all the traditional rites had been completed an old man told me to follow the woman who had brought me to my ancestor's tomb back to my father's compound.

By now our family compound was surrounded by a throng of villagers who were all waiting to greet me, but they had also been instructed not to touch me until after I had been welcomed to my father's house in the traditional manner. Forming a procession, they sang songs as my father sprinkled water around me, welcomed me home and led me into one of the big huts where he asked me to sit on a riempie-seat chair.

People now crowded in to welcome me in true Sudanese fashion. The women knelt in front of me and held both my hands, kissing them. Then they blessed me by kissing my head. The elderly men and women, the only persons who, according to Dinka custom, had the authority to do so, sprinkled water on me and blessed me, thanking God and the ancestors for my return. Each person then introduced themselves to me, explaining our relationship and telling me how happy they were to have me back home. Some were old enough to have known me as a baby, while others said they had heard about the lost son called Aher. Everyone was happy, but it was getting hot and crowded inside the hut. Eventually, someone suggested that I sit in the doorway to receive the members of the clan who were still waiting outside to greet me.

But where was my mother? I was longing to see her.

Suddenly a barefoot boy, maybe eight years old, clad in shorts and a vest came rushing towards the hut, clutching a playing stick. His stick went flying over the head of the woman kneeling in front of me as he jumped onto my lap and hid his face in my shirt. I put my arm round him to comfort him. "That's your brother, Thokriel, Aher," a voice from the crowd said.

My brother? I didn't even know that I had a younger brother!

Still holding Thokriel I got up from the chair and lifted his head. His eyes were red and his lips were trembling. Had this brother of mine missed me too, even though he had been born a decade after my disappearance? I had promised my father that I would be strong, but I cried for joy. "Thokriel!" I said, wiping the tears from his face and mine.

"You have three brothers and two sisters," someone told me. "You will meet your brothers, Majok and Atem, soon. Atem is the eldest. Achel and Ajith are your sisters. There are six of you. And, of course, there is your grandmother, your father's mother. Her name is Awutdit."

"But where is my mother?" I finally asked.

"Looking for you," someone said.

Apparently, the day before, she had been in her own village, but she had heard about my arrival and guessed that I would come straight home. She had walked all night to be in time to welcome me, but when, in the early morning hours, I still hadn't returned she had set off for the airstrip at Turalei. She would be back soon, my relatives assured me.

Holding Thokriel I grew calm again. For now I had a brother to love. And my mother was on her way.

It was about four o'clock when I went down to the river with Thokriel and some elders. I was kneeling to put my hand in the water when I heard voices calling: "Aher! Aher! Your mother's coming!"

"There!" my brother said, pointing.

And there she was, coming from the direction of my grand-mother's village.

People were pouring from their huts to watch. I heard exclamations of joy.

Then I started running. I ran to regain my lost world. I ran over the dry sorghum stalks towards a mother's love.

I knew it was my mother. She was running too.

The next moment my mother was holding me.

Epilogue

"There is no peace in this country, my son, and no safe place for you," my father said to me after I had been living with them in the family compound for a few days. "The war, which once robbed us of you, our son, may now destroy you. Please return to the place where you preserved yourself for us. Live your life in peace, further your studies and prepare yourself to bring us a bright future once peace has come to this land."

When I went in search of my parents in 2002 I never thought about brothers and sisters, but now I had a proper family and I was concerned about the lack of education in their area. I spent forty-eight days with my family before boarding a plane for Lokichokio, accompanied by my two brothers, Majok and Thokriel. Lack of money and proper documentation prevented me from taking them with me to South Africa, so we spent part of 2003 and 2004 in Ifo, where I prepared them for their future education. I bought a blackboard and some chalk and taught them their ABC and 123. I told them about my struggle to obtain an education and lectured them on the importance of learning. It all took careful planning as I had never taken responsibility for anyone else before, and I had to keep moving between Ifo and Nairobi, looking for sponsors and educational materials – comic books or anything else they could read in English. Then, when the three of us decided that they were ready, I took them to Nairobi and enrolled them at a boarding school.

At last I was able to relax. I returned to South Africa at the end of 2004 – this time crossing the borders with an official document – and spent Christmas in Cape Town with a friend, Daniel Deng.

In February 2005 Ma Sannie came to pick me up at a bus stop in Pretoria. I had been racking my brains as to how I would survive and pay for my brothers' education, but when I visited Wonderboom station again, I was relieved to find that my former space was still available and I could resume my business, selling clothes and other items. In July I enrolled for an LLB degree at the University of South Africa. With hard work I am determined to succeed.

My brothers continue to be my inspiration and it is for their sake that I always do my best. Not long after I had returned to South Africa I transferred Majok to St Peter's Primary School, Nsamibya in Kampala, Uganda, where, at the end of 2007, he sat his Primary School Certificate and passed with an aggregate that was among the best in the country. Thokriel, too, did well in Kenya and has now joined Majok in Kampala, where he is due to write his final primary school examination soon.

As for Sudan, a comprehensive peace agreement between the Arab government in the north and the people of the south was signed in 2005, but it did not end the suffering in southern Sudan. And in the west, in Darfur, in the aftermath of this agreement, a horrific genocide took thousands of lives and displaced millions of people.

It saddens me that people who all profess to serve God – calling Him the Almighty in English, Allah in Arabic and Nhialic in Dinka – seem unable to make peace among themselves. I am overcome by a sense of emptiness when I see the conditions the people of Sudan endure and the wars, poverty and diseases they are subject to – conditions that are caused by envy, religious bigotry, racism and cultural ignorance. In every religion there are those who see themselves as superior to others – whether they are richer, or of a worthier skin colour, culture or religious persuasion.

Human beings with less power, they arrogantly believe, are not really important. It is this rejection of others that has for many centuries caused wars in Sudan. The final victory in the Sudanese struggle would have to be the liberation of the minds of the people of Sudan. This liberation would be led by men and women who would have to make a conscious effort to heal and release broken minds and restore the spirit of the country.

Is this ever going to happen? Will the bright future my parents long for ever arrive? Will we, the people of the south, ever resolve our own bloody tribal rivalries and stop the rampant corruption that plagues our society?

A tale is told in Sudan of four animals – a lion, a hyena, a snake and a cheetah – who once shared a hut in a small village. They lived in perfect harmony until they decided that they needed rules. Rules would enable them to be more considerate towards one another. So they held a meeting where each was asked to share his wishes with the others. Snake was first. "I am pleased to say that I have no problem with anyone," he said. "But it is important that we should understand one another, so I'll tell you the one thing I hate, and that is to be touched, even by mistake. If anyone touches me, I'll go to war with him."

Then it was Lion's turn, and he said, "I, too, am happy to be a member of this community and you are welcome to do whatever you want, but there is one thing that I cannot stand and that is noise. If anyone makes a noise, no matter who he is, I will punish him."

"I have nothing to add, but this," Cheetah said: "What I detest more than anything else is meeting someone's eye. So please make sure that you never look me in the eye or there will be trouble!"

Finally, it was Hyena's turn. "I agree to respect the rules the three of you have put forward to protect your rights as free members of this community," he told them. "Everything is fine. Now here are my rules: I will always be coming home late, and when I do, I don't want anyone to ask me where I have been or what I have been doing. That is all I ask of you."

The meeting ended amicably, with all the animals agreeing to implement the rules and consider the rights of their brothers.

Then one night Hyena went hunting and came limping home in the small hours, howling and laughing as hyenas do. He found the other members of the household sleeping quietly in their corners. As he was stumbling towards his bed, complaining about the pain in his joints after his long walk, Lion woke up. "What's that noise?" Lion roared. "What are you doing? Where have you been all night? Who gave you the right to disturb us at this hour?"

"Don't you dare ask me questions!" Hyena retorted angrily. "Where I have been and what I was doing is none of your business! Keep your paws off me!"

Lion rose and growled, but Hyena was ready to protect his own rights and the two animals fought fiercely until they tripped over Snake, who was sleeping in his corner. Snake reared up and bit both fighters.

When morning came, and Cheetah woke, the three were still at it. Then, suddenly, it dawned on them that there might be an honourable solution. Cheetah was uninvolved! He could be the arbitrator. Peace negotiations commenced. Lion, Snake and Hyena each explained their grievances. Cheetah was about to speak, when he caught the three of them looking at him expectantly, waiting to hear his verdict. "Why are you all staring at me?" he exploded. "I told you never to meet my eye!"

So the judge joined the renewed fighting and each animal continued to battle for his own rights, until, much later, the exhausted warriors escaped to separate spots in the bush for shelter and protection.

That is how Lion, Cheetah, Snake and Hyena came to live in separate villages. Their negotiations and their laws had made it impossible for them ever to live together in peace.

Acknowledgements

I owe my life to God. I thank the Almighty for giving me the courage and strength that carried me through all my endeavours.

My gratitude to Sannie Meiring for her unwavering guidance and support. I am indebted to her for so much. Without her kind assistance I could not have written this book. May God bless her.

My respect and thanks to my friend Daniel Jok Mading, for treating me with understanding and confidentiality, for inspiring me with his courage, for always being there for me.

My appreciation to the two men, one from the DRC and one from Bangladesh, who befriended me on the bus ride to Malawi. They will never know how much I value their contribution to my success.

Thanks to the Meiring family in South Africa for embracing me, especially to Rykie Meiring, Piet Meiring, Mientjie Preller and Sorien van Garderen. You have brought me love and hope.

To my own family – my two grandmothers, Awut Kuacnyuel (my father's mother) and Ajok Majok Adiang (my mother's mother), my father, Arop Bol, and my mother, Dot Atem Majak – thank you for welcoming me back to the home of my great ancestors.

Uncle Atem Bol, who took me to the refugee camp in Ethiopia – you saved my life.

Riak Atem and Aker Bol Majok, I will remember you for putting me in touch with my lost family.

My brothers, Thokriel and Majok, it is for you that I keep working. I am proud of you and your success. Keep up the good work!

To all my friends, Leuth Buk Atem, Lemson Chikwiriro and others – I salute you! I appreciate what you have done for me. We will continue our journey through life with care and honour and perseverance, in memory of our friendship. Not to forget Aunty Elizabeth Aguek Mangok, who died in a plane crash in 2007, for her warm assistance when I stayed in her house in Nairobi with my brothers. May her soul rest in peace.

Bol Deng Tach, long ago in Panyido camp you taught me my alphabet. I wish I could show you the book I have now written. Many thanks, too, to all the other teachers who have inspired me, people like Mr Ndoro, headmaster of Visitation High School (Makumbi Mission), his deputy and staff.

To the Kwela crew, Nicola Menné, Nèlleke de Jager, Wendy Hendricks and Ettie Williams, who have done so much to polish and publish *The Lost Boy*, thank you! And last but not least, to Antjie Krog and Johanna Mennen, who believed in the manuscript enough to pass it on.